RATH OCT 25 '00

D0938571

796.357 FEH
FEHLER, GENE, 1940-
TALES FROM BASEBALL'S
GOLDEN AGE /

DEMCO

# Tales from Baseball's Golden Age

## Gene Fehler

Sports Publishing Inc.
www.SportsPublishingInc.com

© 2000 by Gene Fehler
All Rights Reserved.

Director of Production: Susan M. McKinney
Book design: Jennifer Polson
Book layout: Jay Peterson and Jennifer Polson
Dustjacket design: Christina Cary

Photo credits: Brace Photo, Chicago, IL: pp. 3, 7, 15, 26, 59, 79, 92, 143, 158, 165, 177, 195, 223, 241, 252; SPI Archives: pp. 35, 48, 70, 110, 123, 135, 185.

ISBN: 1-58261-247-1


SPORTS PUBLISHING INC.
804 North Neil
Champaign, IL 61820
www.sportspublishinginc.com

Printed in the United States of America.

*For Lew Frosch and Johnny Creighton,
for those thousands of hours
of 1950s baseball joys we shared.*

# ACKNOWLEDGMENTS

My deepest thanks to the players who gave me the gift of their time and their enthusiasm in sharing with me these recollections of their careers. Without their generosity there could be no book.

To Mike Schacht, editor of *Fan* magazine, where many of the pieces about Ted Williams originally appeared.

To my late grandfather, John Ashpole, and my late father, Franklin Fehler. My love of baseball had its origins in those radio broadcasts they listened to—my grandfather's Cubs and my dad's White Sox.

To my mom, Hazel Fehler, who has always given me encouragement—and thankfully had the vision to give me *The Official Encyclopedia of Baseball* by Hy Turkin and S.C. Thompson when I was 11 years old, bringing me my first delicious taste of baseball's history and statistics.

To my sisters—Jan Bradley, Rita Badger, and Rhonda Fehler—three special women.

To my sons, Andy and Tim; my daughters-in-law, Misty and Jacquelyn; my grandaughter, Mireille; and my mother-in-law, Charlotte Eggert.

To my wife and best friend, Polly. Thanks.

# CONTENTS

# Preface

One theme rings loud and clear in the voices of the players of the '40s and '50s: a love of the game. Oh, they'll admit to being willing to accept more money, should it have been offered them. They acknowledge the need to play hurt and to feeling the pressure of losing their job to one of the numerous eager minor leaguers. They recall long, hot doubleheaders, a menu of inside fastballs, sleepless nights on trains. Yet, as with one voice, they express the joy of having been there. Here's a sampling of how the players feel about having been a part of the '50s Golden Age of Baseball.

*Cal Abrams:* I played my heart out wherever I played. We played back then because we loved the game. I'd do it all over again. I'd ride the buses. Baseball's the greatest thing that ever happened to me.

*Andy Carey:* I treasure just having the opportunity to play baseball in New York in the '50s. It was probably the best city in the world to be in in those days. Bauer and I used to go downtown and then come back through Harlem and wave at Campanella in the store. We'd go out to nightclubs in Harlem in those days. It was a good town, it was a fun town; obviously, you were on the top of the world. I mean, you couldn't be any higher than playing in New York back in the '50s and to have participated in the number of Series that I have, to have been involved with Hall of Famers—to have played with Yogi Berra, Enos Slaughter, Johnny Mize, Phil Rizzuto, Mickey Mantle, Bill Dickey—you know, Hall of Famers. Casey Stengel, a Hall of Famer. I mean, not many people get opportunities like that in their lifetime.

*Sonny Dixon:* I was so very lucky to be able to play in the big leagues with the other 200 men in the American League when it was a game and you played for the love of the game. In my book each player was great, and I was a lucky one.

*Ferris Fain:* I'm sure there was more true enjoyment in playing baseball in the '50s. We didn't have the money to worry about. We didn't have free agency that makes players look ahead two or three years and wonder where they will be playing and worrying about injuries that might keep them from big money. For me, the competition was everything. I just enjoyed the thrill of it. I was getting paid to do something I loved to do. If I had a good day, that's wonderful; if I didn't, I wasn't going to jump off the bridge. I loved getting out in the afternoon, getting out on the freshly cut lawn. Every day was a different game.

*Gail Harris:* The thing that I treasure the most was being able to see the players and play against the players in both leagues there in the mid-to-late '50s. 'Cause with being with the Giants in the National League and of course with the Tigers over in the American League I got to play against the Musials and the Mantles and the Aarons and the Williamses and the whole crew. There's not enough money to buy a Mays or a Mantle on the open market today.

*Herb Plews:* I always felt lucky to have played the game during some of the game's finest years. In spite of our record I was proud to represent our nation's capital.

*J.W. Porter:* I'm so proud to have been a player in the '50s that I could explode. Oh, I wish I could have played more, done a little better. But I was there. Of all those kids at Oakland Tech who wanted to be, I was the one that was. It's a side room, that American Legion room in the Hall of Fame at Cooperstown, but I'm there. Rollie Fingers is in both rooms. Wow! I hit a homer off Don Larsen the next April after his perfect World Series game. Double wow!

*Carl Scheib:* I treasure the fact that I got to play in the big leagues against good competition. I get an awful lot of autograph letters from elderly people, and they all say those are the best years they can remember in baseball. And I think it is, because in those years they had more fan and player associations together, and idols.

*Charlie Silvera:* I played with and roomed with many Hall of Famers, played in New York in the greatest era with the greatest team and met the finest people that anyone would want to meet in their lifetime.

*Wayne Terwilliger:* I think the biggest thing about my career is that I got the chance to play against all the great players, with and against them. I look back and I think, Geez, I played with and against some of the greatest players that ever played this game, for crying out loud. I didn't do a heck of a lot, but I did little things, you know. I got home runs off Whitey Ford, a Hall of Famer. Don Newcombe. I look back on some of the guys—Jim Bunning. I took Jim Bunning downtown. I can look back at those and I can laugh about it, but I had a great time.

*Frank Thomas:* Baseball meant everything to me. I played in an era that I think will go down in history as the greatest era in baseball.

*Gus Zernial:* I look at when I played, with the DiMaggios and the Henrichs and the Mantles and New York with the Raschis and Reynolds and the pitching and take a look at Boston with Williams and Bobby Doerr and Stephens. We had some outstanding ballplayers. We were coming back off a world war and a lot of the players were just coming into their own and the public accepted them and they became heroes. Real heroes. I think the era of the '50s came off that, with those kind of individuals. Really and truly, I think the fans knew that we were playing to please them.

# Cal Abrams

Eight years (1949–1956)
Born: March 2, 1924  BL  TL  6'0"  185 lbs.
Positions: Outfield, 440; 1B, 4
Brooklyn Dodgers, Cincinnati Reds, Pittsburgh Pirates,
Baltimore Orioles, Chicago White Sox

| G | BA | AB | H | 2B | 3B | HR | R | RBI | BB | SO | SB | FA |
|---|----|----|---|----|----|----|---|-----|----|----|----|----|
| 567 | .269 | 1611 | 433 | 64 | 19 | 32 | 257 | 138 | 304 | 90 | 12 | .977 |

*Cal's being thrown out at home in the last of the ninth inning at Brooklyn in 1950 remains a key moment in baseball history. His run would have forced a playoff. Instead, the Phillies won the game, and the pennant, in the 10th inning on Dick Sisler's home run. In four full minor league seasons (1946–1949), Cal hit .331, .345, .337, and .336, scoring over 100 runs each season. In 1953, he hit .286 with 15 home runs in 119 games for Pittsburgh. In 1954, he hit .293 in 115 games for Baltimore. He was involved in the 1952 trade that sent Gus*

Bell from Pittsburgh to the Reds. In 1954, he was traded
to Baltimore for Dick Littlefield. In 1955, he went to the
White Sox for infielder Bobby Adams.

## *Jocko's Honesty*

[A National League umpire from 1941 to 1965,
Jocko Conlan was elected to the Baseball Hall of Fame
in 1974.]

We're playing in the Polo Grounds and it's pouring
rain. Ninth inning, bases loaded, three-and-two
on me, and they're beating us by one run. The Barber,
Sal Maglie, is pitching, and everybody's screaming in
the rain, and Sal threw a curveball three-and-two. I
knew it was high. The ball went over my shoulder and
down into the catcher's mitt, and this is the way Jocko Conlin
called it: "Strike three, let's get out of here, it's raining."

I turned around and said, "Jocko," my face pouring with water, "tell me the truth." He said, "You
know it was a ball, but let's get out of here."

And that was the end of that. To me, there's such a
significance to that. The fact that this man could tell
me this. Jocko, with certain Irish feeling about him—to
me, it was like the Irishman and the Jewish man were
getting together.

I was very relieved, and I said, "Ah, ha, it was a
ball, so I would have walked and tied the score."

*Cal Abrams*

# *Happy Felton*

At Brooklyn, Happy Felton had his pregame radio show. A player would play ball with three kids. The one who the player chose as the best player got to talk to a player in the dugout, and the player got 50 dollars. Snider and Hodges made about a thousand dollars a year from playing with the kids and talking to them in the dugout.

I got asked one time to play with the kids. Fifty dollars. So I said to this one kid, "I'm going to choose you, no matter how you do. Now, when they ask you who you want to talk to, say, 'Cal Abrams.'" I figured I'd make an extra 50 dollars.

When we were done playing, they asked me which kid won. I lied and named this kid. But when they asked him who he wanted to talk to in the dugout, he told them, "Jackie Robinson."

The fans in Ebbets Field were great. The kids used to mill around Rotunda and get autographs on penny postcards. One kid came to me every day for three weeks, getting my autograph. Finally, I got a little curious and asked him, "Why do you want to keep getting my autograph?"

He said, "I need 21 Cal Abrams to trade for a Jackie Robinson."

# Johnny Berardino

11 years (1939–1942, 1946–1952)
Born: May 1, 1917   BR   TR   5'11 1/2"   175 lbs.
Positions: 2B, 453; SS, 266; 3B, 91; 1B, 26; OF, 1
St. Louis Browns, Cleveland Indians, Pittsburgh Pirates

| G | BA | AB | H | 2B | 3B | HR | R | RBI | BB | SO | SB | FA |
|-----|------|------|-----|-----|-----|-----|-----|-----|-----|-----|-----|------|
| 912 | .249 | 3028 | 755 | 167 | 23 | 36 | 334 | 387 | 284 | 268 | 27 | .960 |

*B*erardino entered Southern California University on a football scholarship, intending to play quarterback, but played baseball instead. He signed with the St. Louis Browns after his second year at USC, where he led the conference in hitting. Signed as a second baseman, he played primarily shortstop with the Browns in 1940 and '41. In 1940, he hit 16 home runs and drove in 95 runs. In 1941, he dropped to five home runs, yet drove in 89 runs. *He spent 1943-1945 in the military. He had a unique career; in his last three seasons, he played for the same three teams twice each, in the same order: Browns, Indians, Pirates, Browns, Indians, Pirates. He was traded to the Indians in 1947 and played 50 games for the Indians in their world-championship season in 1948. A child actor, he returned to acting after his baseball career ended, taking the role of Dr. Steve Hardy on the television soap opera* General Hospital *in 1963 and playing it for more than 30 years.*

## Secret Streak

Nowadays they start announcing consecutive-game hitting streaks when they reach five or six games. When I was with the Browns, I hit in 22 straight games, but nobody knew it but my roommate and me, because I told him.

*Johnny Berardino*

# The Double Date

Ted Williams and I went up to the majors the same year, in '39, and in his first visit to St. Louis I asked him if he wanted to go out one night, double-date, and he said, "Yeah."

So, to explain how things were much different then, I got him a date and got me a date and we went out and had hamburgers and milk shakes and we took the girls home and went to bed.

Alone.

# Spike Wound

I got spiked by Joe DiMaggio on my ankle and I treasure the scar.

# Jimmy Bloodworth

11 years (1937, 1939–1943, 1946–1947, 1949–1951)
Born: July 26, 1917  BR  TR  5'11"  180 lbs.
Positions: 2B, 867; 1B, 53; 3B, 22; OF, 5; SS, 3
Washington Senators, Detroit Tigers, Pittsburgh Pirates,
Cincinnati Reds, Philadelphia Phillies

| G | BA | AB | H | 2B | 3B | HR | R | RBI | BB | SO | SB | FA |
|---|-----|------|-----|-----|----|----|-----|-----|-----|-----|----|------|
| 1002 | .248 | 3519 | 874 | 160 | 20 | 62 | 347 | 453 | 200 | 407 | 19 | .976 |

*B*loodworth batted .289 for the Senators in 1939, his first full season. A steady performer, he played in over a hundred games during his next four seasons, batting between .241 and .245 each year. He hit a career-high 13 home runs in 1942. After two years in the military, he played in more than 100 games only once, hitting .261 in 134 games for the Reds in 1949, including an 8-for-14 mark as a pinch hitter. He was traded with Doc Cramer to *the Tigers in 1941 for Frank Croucher and Bruce Campbell.*

## *Playing Baseball*

I treasure my baseball memories.

I had open-heart surgery, and it was my baseball memories that helped me through it. While I was sick and recuperating and all, I'd start thinking about a certain ball game and just play it all the way through, think about it all the way through.

Sometimes I'd work up a sweat, and Doc asked me, "Do you have a fever?" and I told him, "No, I've just been playing baseball."

He told me, "That old heart won't stand much of that."

## *Lou Gehrig Day*

I remember the first ball game I ever played in the big leagues in 1937. The first time I went to bat, I hit against Lefty Grove. He was one of the greats. That was quite a thrill. Then in 1939 I was in Yankee Stadium and played in the ball game when they had Lou Gehrig Day, on July 4. That will always be the outstanding event in my baseball career, to see all those old former

Yankees. I played against Lou Gehrig in 1937 also. To see him in 1939 kind of made me feel real bad, made me realize a lot of things what could and will happen to us.

They had all the 1927 Yankees, supposed to be one of the greatest ball clubs ever assembled, and there was Babe Ruth and Earle Combs, and all the old living ballplayers were all standing out on the pitcher's mound. When Lou Gehrig made a talk, they all came up and greeted him. To see all those old ballplayers like that, it was kind of a thrill, but then it was real sad also. But it was one of the most outstanding events I've ever seen. I heard on several different occasions that the fire department had given the Yankee management permission to let people sit in the aisles that day. It was full of people, I'll tell you. I thought it was going to burst the sides out of Yankee stadium.

## *Cabbage Leaves*

One August we played a ball game in St. Louis, Missouri. I weighed around 178-180 pounds. Cecil Travis was big. He wasn't real heavyset, but I guess he weighed 190 pounds. We played a doubleheader, and he and I were the only two ballplayers on the ball club that played two nine-inning ball games. We had pitchers in the outfield. Man, it was hot.

We took a green cabbage and put it in ice water and we'd take a leaf off it and put it in our cap when we ran out on the field. That's insulation for your brain. Then we'd change it, put it back in the ice water and get another one. But when we came off the field, the trainer met us with some smelling salts and a wet sponge. We walked off the field, we couldn't trot off. And we just sat down.

In fact, they put a stool in the shower and Travis went in and sat down with his uniform on. The uniforms were flannel. They were hot and heavy. Boy, they were heavy! But, then, that's all we knew then.

We were just about gone. That was the hottest day I've ever seen in baseball.

# *Yogi Berra*

A lot of the catchers would talk to you, ask you what to hit, just to try to break your concentration. They'd talk to you.

That darn Yogi Berra. You went up there to hit when he was catching, he'd be talking to you and throwing sand in your shoes. Throw it up there. You'd get out and shake it and try to make him quit, and the umpire couldn't see it, of course. And when you got on base or got out you'd have to stop and dump the sand out of your shoes.

# Ray Boone

13 years (1948–1960)
Born: July 27, 1923   BR  TR  6'  172 lbs.
Positions: 3B, 510; SS, 464; 1B, 285; 2B, 1
Cleveland Indians, Detroit Tigers, Chicago White Sox,
Kansas City Athletics, Milwaukee Braves, Boston Red Sox

| G | BA | AB | H | 2B | 3B | HR | R | RBI | BB | SO | SB | FA |
|---|----|----|---|----|----|----|---|-----|----|----|----|----|
| 1373 | .275 | 4589 | 1260 | 162 | 461 | 51 | 645 | 737 | 608 | 463 | 21 | .966 |

*B*oone was named to two All-Star teams, in 1954 and 1956. He led the American League with 116 RBI in 1955. A catcher in his first minor league season at Wausau, he batted .306. As a shortstop in the Texas League, he was hitting .355 in 87 games when he was called up to Cleveland to replace Lou Boudreau on the pennant-winning Indians. He hit .301 for Cleveland in 1950 and .308 for Detroit in 1956. He hit 20 or more home runs in four straight years. Ray is the father of former major league catcher and manager, Bob, and grandfather of major league players, Bret and Aaron.

## We're Talking Baseball

Pitchers don't get into the ball game as much as your regular players, your catchers in particular. Especially the starters, who pitch every fourth day or something like that. When I was with Detroit, me and the infielder would be just talking and the pitcher would walk up, and I always use to kid them and say, "Hey, we're talking baseball here."

## DiMaggio's Charisma

We played the Yankees in a lot of important series. My first trip in there with Cleveland, I was playing catch with Hank Majeski before the game and I'm kind of in awe of the stadium. It looked like there was going to be a big crowd there, they were starting to come in early. The Yankees were taking batting practice, and all of a sudden this roar goes up. Of course, I look around, wondering what happened. Hank Majeski

**Ray Boone**

walked out to me and said, "Joe D just came out of the dugout."

Then he proceeded to tell me that Joe DiMaggio always stayed in the dugout when the regulars started hitting, and if he was third that day, as soon as the second man went in to hit, well, the crowd knew that Joe D would come out of the dugout, and as soon as they saw that Yankee hat, this roar went up.

I thought, "Man, that's pretty good."

He had that kind of charisma about him.

# A Helpful Yogi

Whenever Cleveland played the Yankees on a Sunday afternoon in Yankee Stadium, you had a full house. They had a big black tarp out there in dead center field. Well, they would drop that on Sunday afternoon and put fans out there. When they'd put those fans out there, well, they'd all have those white shirts on. It made a real lousy background. When you went to bat, Yogi was first to remind you of the background. He said, "Boy, tough background today."

# Tommy Byrne

13 years (1943, 1946–1957)
Born: December 31, 1919   BL   TL   6'1"   182 lbs.
Position: Pitcher
New York Yankees, St. Louis Browns, Chicago White Sox,
Washington Senators

| G | W | L | PCT | ERA | GS | CG | SV | IP | H | BB | SO | BA | FA |
|---|---|---|-----|-----|----|----|----|----|----|----|----|----|----|
| 281 | 85 | 69 | .552 | 4.11 | 70 | 65 | 12 | 1362 | 1138 | 1037 | 766 | .238 | .943 |

*B*yrne won 15 or more games three times with the
Yankees. He had 12 career shutouts. In 1955 he led
the league with a .762 winning percentage, going 16-5.
He led the league in walks in 1949, '50, and '51. He led
the league in hit batsmen five times. In 1942 he went 17-
4 for Newark of the International League despite leading
the league in walks. In 1954 he went 20-10 for Seattle of
the Pacific Coast League and led the league in strikeouts.

*He finished the year with the Yankees, where he completed four of his five starts, going 3-2 with a 2.70 ERA. One of baseball's top-hitting pitchers, he batted .263 as a pitcher. A 6-for-80 mark as a pinch hitter lowered his career batting average to .238. He hit 14 career home runs, eight triples, and 26 doubles. He pitched in six World Series games, going 1-1 with a 2.53 ERA. He played on four Yankee pennant-winning teams and two World Series winners.*

## Casey, Changing Pitchers

I was pitching against the Athletics one day at Yankee Stadium. It was in the fifth inning, and we had them 5-2. With two outs, after a bunch of foul balls, I walked the bases loaded. Gus Zernial is coming up to hit. Well, Casey came running out of the dugout, and he hadn't even crossed the chalk line yet and he's waving to the bullpen for the right-hander.

I said, "Wait a minute! Wait a minute!" I'm yelling at him. You know, I felt great. I had good stuff. They couldn't hit it, so that's the only reason we hadn't got them out. They'd just walk after they fouled off pitches.

And he says, "No, I'm going to make a change. I'm going to make a change."

I said, "Change, my butt." You know, I very rarely got mad out there.

He said, "Give me the ball."

18

I said, "No, I'm not going to give you the ball." And I kicked the rosin bag halfway to second base. And he's following me, see, he's going up on the mound, now he's going down the mound, and we're halfway to second base.

He says, "You know why I'm taking you out?"

I said, "Heck, no. It was nothing-nothing when we started and we're winning 5-2 now."

And he said, "I'm afraid you're going to hurt somebody."

He thought that was funny, but it wasn't funny to me. I had already hit four guys, and I had hit Ferris Fain twice. But the point was, he said that jokingly, thinking that would be something to cool me down a little bit. And I saw this pitcher coming in—Fred Sanford, coming in from right field, and he was halfway between [right fielder] Hank Bauer and [second baseman] Jerry Coleman and I threw the ball over Coleman's head and it hit Sanford right at the belt.

I said, "Did you see that, Casey?"

He said, "Yeah, I saw it."

And I said, "It was a strike."

And I walked off the mound. Well, when I walked off the mound, then he got real angry.

I went in and sat down in the dugout. It's got numbers where the guys hang their jackets, you know, and 37 is where he'd sit. Well, I sat in his place, and he gave Sanford the pep talk. When he came in from the mound, I wouldn't get up. He sat down right next to me, and I didn't say anything and he didn't say anything. After a couple or three pitches, Zernial doubled and tied the score. After that inning was over, I went on in and took my shower and listened to it on the radio. It went on to the 11th inning and we got beat.

Everybody came in there pretty much upset that we blew the game.

Casey yelled to Pete Sheehy, the clubhouse man, "Call everybody in the center of the clubhouse."

Casey went in and threw his hat down. He had his shirt half-buttoned, unbuttoned, his pants half down, and he was mad. But this was good. You know, you've got to get upset.

He looked around at everybody and he said, "The next time I go to the mound and make a pitching change, the guy I'm taking out, we'll both walk in together." And I didn't get the inference to that, other than the fact that I did act like an idiot.

But what probably happened was that the fans evidently applauded some for me when I came off the field, maybe because I was showing my butt, I don't know. But then when he came in, they obviously booed; but sitting back in the dugout, I didn't hear it. I mean, ballplayers don't think of that, or don't hear that, you know, but Casey could hear it. And he was telling me in a nice way that we weren't going to do any of that crap again.

But Casey was a good man. We got along fine. He was left-handed and I understood him and he understood me.

# A Good Boy

Yogi talked to everybody behind the plate. In fact, I was always accusing him later, "That guy hit that ball pretty good. Are you telling him what's coming?"

He says, "Heck, no, I ain't telling him what's coming." He says, "You're only throwing two pitches. You've got to guess good once."

This was in the earlier years. But Yogi, he'd talk to them about anything. It was like he hadn't seen them in six years. They're coming up to home plate the first time in a game, and he'd take his mask off and he'd kick his heels against his shin guards and even meet them.

I said, "When you going to shake hands with them?"

But he's really trying to do his thing and get them thinking about something else. Which is pretty good. He had a way with folks and he still has. He's a good boy.

# The Artist, Eddie Lopat

Lopat threw a screwball and a slow curve. He'd turn his fastball over like a screwball, and yet he had a good fastball because of the junk he threw. A lot of times they wouldn't swing at it because it was such a surprise to them. But he could make them swing at a pitch they really didn't want to hit. He'd throw it to them and make it look big by changing speeds, and it would take a long time to get there, and they'd want to hit it, but they couldn't hit it out of the park very well. He would only throw maybe 80 or 95 pitches a game.

In hot summer, he'd say, "Put your hand under my arm." It'd be the sixth or seventh inning, and he wouldn't even be sweating. And I'd have to go out and pitch the second game and I'd change my uniform in the third inning. It'd be wringing wet.

He was probably as talented as any pitcher I believe I've ever known for his God-given talent. He was an artist. There are a lot of tricks in the trade, and I probably copied myself after him in the last three or four years I pitched. I pitched to let them hit it, but not too far—let them hit it where I wanted them to hit it, to get double plays and stuff. Lopat was very clever in his work.

## *Pitch According to the Umpire*

The way I see it, you're pitching according to the umpire. In other words, it seems to me that some umpires have a tendency to favor the outside part of the plate or the inside part of the plate. If your ball's going away and it's three inches outside the plate when the guy catches it and the umpire calls it a strike—man, that never happened to me before—but I think I'd try to throw it there again. If I got it one time . . . you know what I mean?

This thing about running out on the mound with a bat in your hand, and you're going to hit the pitcher with it and all that stuff—man, all I'd do is ask Yogi to throw me the darn ball back and I'd hit him again.

# On the Threshold of Greatness

I lived on the threshold of maybe being pretty good, but I was wild. The strike zone, the further up you go in baseball, gets smaller and smaller. I was off the plate a lot, and I led the league two or three years in a row in bases on balls and hit batsmen. [Byrne led the American League in bases on balls from 1949 to 1951.] I did manage to get a raise every year, though, because I was prone to win a few games.

I always told the ball club, "If you get some people on and let me get my three or four cuts, we'll get some runs." And although I had great stuff and all, not many of them wanted to hit at me, you know?

# *Mickey Mantle*

Mickey had God-given talent in a lot of various areas. He was the fastest thing at that time that I recall in baseball. He could literally fly. He had great power from either side of the plate. He had a good arm. I really believe he's probably one of the greatest athletes I've ever seen. I think he could have been heavyweight champion of the world if he'd wanted to be. And I know he could have won an Olympic medal in sprinting, or 100 meters or something, 'cause he could fly. And I believe he could have made an All-Pro football player because, once he made the corner, I don't think anybody could have come close to catching him.

# Andy Carey

11 years (1952–1962)
Born: October 18, 1931   BR   TR   6'1 1/2"   190 lbs.
Position: Third Base
New York Yankees, Kansas City Athletics,
Chicago White Sox, Los Angeles Dodgers

| G | BA | AB | H | 2B | 3B | HR | R | RBI | BB | SO | SB | FA |
|---|----|----|---|----|----|----|---|-----|----|----|----|-----|
| 938 | .260 | 2850 | 741 | 119 | 38 | 64 | 371 | 350 | 268 | 389 | 23 | .957 |

*A* $60,000 Yankee bonus baby, Carey played in four consecutive World Series, 1955–1958. He hit .302 in 1954. In 1955 he led the American League with 11 triples. He tied a major league record for third basemen with four double plays in a 1955 game. He played third base behind Don Larsen during Larsen's perfect game in the 1956 World Series. Carey was with the Yankees from 1952 until 1960, when he was traded to the Athletics for Bob Cerv.*

*Andy Carey*

# *Don Larsen's Perfect Game*

I wish I still had that newspaper, one of two different ones my dad had printed at a shop in Times Square the night before Don's perfect game. "Larsen Pitches No-Hitter Against Dodgers," the headline read, some 18 hours before Don took the mound for real. Dad took both papers back to his apartment at the Concourse Plaza Hotel, then put the "No-Hit" paper on Don's door for him to find in the morning.

Back in his room, Dad had second thoughts; maybe the newspaper would jinx Don. Dad retrieved it, then destroyed it—his contribution to history. I'm glad I still have that other newspaper with its headline: "Goonybird Wins 5th Game." "Goonybird" was the affectionate nickname Dad, who had been Don's close friend for several years, had given him because of Don's slow nature. Dad almost got rid of that newspaper, too, then decided to keep it as a souvenir to show Don if he won.

He won, all right, in a game filled with images I will always remember: the no-windup delivery that Bob Turley had been first to use and that Don had been experimenting with for a month; the line drive by Hodges that I caught about four inches off the ground to my left; Hodges' earlier line drive to left-center that Mantle ran down—a spectacular catch; Robinson's liner off my glove, deflected to McDougald at short, his great play to throw out Robinson by a hair at first. I still have a picture of the called out at first, truly a matter of inches, Robinson's foot about a foot from first when Collins caught the ball. The same play had occurred at least twice during the course of the season with the same results, perhaps a dress rehearsal to history.

We were aware of the no-hitter in progress, but as usual in baseball, we weren't talking about it (one of baseball's most honored superstitions). I think, too, we were more interested in winning the game. Even in the midst of jubilation, it wasn't until afterwards that we all truly realized the significance of Don's feat. According to Don, he was hoping that I was going to play that day, as he always felt I brought him good luck.

I'm glad I played that afternoon—October 8, 1956; good luck was plentiful that day, luck for me and Don and baseball fans everywhere, enough good luck to last all of us for a long time.

## *Finding Religion*

Pitchers back then came in a little bit closer than they do now. Á la Drysdale, you know. He'd make a Christian out of you.

# Bubba Church

Six years (1950–1955)
Born: September 12, 1924   BR   TR   6'0"   180 lbs.
Position: Pitcher
Philadelphia Phillies, Cincinnati Reds, Chicago Cubs

| G | W | L | PCT | ERA | GS | CG | SV | IP | H | BB | SO | BA | FA |
|---|---|---|-----|-----|----|----|----|----|----|----|----|----|----|
| 147 | 36 | 37 | .493 | 4.10 | 95 | 32 | 4 | 713.1 | 738 | 274 | 274 | .226 | .950 |

*A* good-hitting pitcher, Church started his career in
1947 with Salina of the Western Association, where
he was 21-9 as a pitcher and also played the outfield. In
1949 he was 15-8 with a league-leading ERA of 2.35 for
Toronto in the International League. In 1950, as a National League rookie, he went 8-6 with a 2.73 ERA and
helped the Philadelphia "Whiz Kids" to the pennant. His
season ended early when he was struck in the face by a Ted

*Kluszewski line drive. In 1951 he had his best season, with a 15-11 mark. In 1952 he was traded to the Reds for Johnny Wyrostek and Kent Peterson. In 1953 he was traded to the Cubs for Fred Baczewski and Bob Kelly.*

## Musial, a Hard Man to Fool

The first time I ever pitched to Musial—I was a young hotshot, and all that kind of stuff. I had a good fastball and had a good curveball and felt like I knew how to pitch. The first pitch I threw him was a strike on the outside corner of the plate. I said, "He can't get around on the ball." Not my fastball. I came back with something else, and I wanted another fastball, and I wanted it right where I threw him the first pitch. Seminick shook it off. I shook him off. In those days the catcher let you throw what you wanted to throw, because it was your ball game. I threw that pitch out there, and Musial hit that darn thing in the upper left-field deck in Shibe Park, but it was about three feet foul. Andy was on his way from behind home plate before it ever got out there, and he said, "Hey, Bubba, you don't throw this guy the same pitch two times in one at-bat. You just don't do it."

Musial beat me two times. He beat me 2-1 in Philadelphia, and he beat me 2-1 in St. Louis. The reason he beat me in Philadelphia was that he hit a fly ball to advance somebody from second to third. And then they scored on an infield ground ball, 2-1. In

St. Louis I got things going real good and I ain't got nothing else to throw him, and I threw him one of my change-ups and he hit it right over the deck in Sportsman's Park.

The next day I said, "Hey, Stan, did you see it coming?"

He said, "Bubba, your motion was too slow, it wasn't your normal motion. I knew what was coming."

## Larry Goetz's Advice

On this particular night I was throwing little bitty baseballs and putting the ball where I wanted to throw it. I think I'm painting the black, but Goetz is calling it a ball. About the third time he called it a ball, I come off the mound and I go toward home plate, and I got something to say, and my catcher Andy Seminick, our Mad Russian, came out there and met me.

He said, "Hey, stop. Don't argue with this guy, he'll throw you—." And Larry Goetz was right behind Andy, and he said, "You—get back on that mound and pitch. It was a ball."

So I went back up there, and I did the best I could do.

The next day Goetz came to me and said, "Hey, Bubba, I want to talk to you."

I said, "Okay." I know I won the ball game; otherwise, I would not have talked to him.

He said, "Let me show you what's happening out there. Coming off the rubber your left foot is going too far to the left, and when the ball gets to home plate, you're looking at it from the first-base side. It looks like a strike to you, but the darn thing is three inches outside. I will not call it a strike."

So I went back over it and looked at it, and you know, the guy was right.

# A Higher Dimension

I found out that if I got a little bit of wax shoe polish on my fingers and then got out to the mound and took the rosin bag, I had a sticky finger. It just helped the rotation on the ball. Now, there was an umpire named Lon Warneke who had pitched for the Cardinals; he knew what it was like out there. Lon carried me into a higher dimension. He said to me, "Ever heard of olive oil? Just picture a glove in your hand and fold your hand around it. Put about four drops of olive oil in the crease, down there on the heel of your hand, and then go out there and sprinkle some rosin on it."

And you ain't seen nothing like it in your life. I've got pictures in my den right now where my fingers are so black from the rosin and the olive oil. You can do anything you want to do with the ball.

# Jerry Coleman

Nine years (1949–1957)
Born: September 14, 1924   BR   TR   6'0"   165 lbs.
Positions: 2B, 572; SS, 116; 3B, 41
New York Yankees

| G | BA | AB | H | 2B | 3B | HR | R | RBI | BB | SO | SB | FA |
|---|----|----|----|----|----|----|----|-----|-----|-----|-----|-----|
| 723 | .263 | 2119 | 558 | 77 | 18 | 16 | 267 | 217 | 235 | 218 | 22 | .973 |

*A*n All-Star in his second season with the Yankees,
Coleman led AL second basemen in fielding his rookie
year. He played in 26 World Series games in six World
Series with the Yankees, hitting .275 with only one error
in 96 chances. Military service cost him three full seasons
during World War II and almost two full seasons in 1952–
1953. After his career, he worked in the Yankee front office
for three years and was a Yankee broadcaster for nine years.

*A longtime broadcaster for the San Diego Padres, he took a one-year sabbatical to manage the team in the 1980 season.*

## A Bad Week

You know what a bad week was? This was a bad week: Trucks, Trout, Hutchinson, Newhouser, Lemon, Feller, Wynn, Garcia. We always got them back-to-back. We always played Detroit and Cleveland back-to-back. That was a rotten week. I still remember, oh, man, except Newhouser, they're all right-handed, and I was a right-handed batter. I still recall, boy, we go from one frying pan into another.

They were all marvelous pitchers. Newhouser's in the Hall of Fame. Lemon, Feller, Wynn are in the Hall of Fame. They could all pitch. And they always came back-to-back. That was a bad week.

## Learning the Hit-and-Run

My greatest strength as a player was my defense. I had a very good arm, and I was a good defensive player. I could make the double play, and that's why the Yankees kept me. I learned to hit-and-run, I could bunt,

*Jerry Coleman*

I could do things to stay alive, and today I see people who don't know how to bunt, they don't even know what the hit-and-run is.

Here's how I learned to hit-and-run. I was 17 years old. World War II had just started, and I wanted to get in the service. I wanted to become a naval aviator, but I couldn't get in until I was 18. I played that summer [1942] for Wellsville, New York, in the Pony League [Coleman hit .304 in 83 games], and our season ended on September 6. My buddy and I decided to keep playing ball during those last days before my birthday on September 14. Then we were going to go down and sign up.

There was an old steel-haired man, tall and lean, down at the ballpark. He had a pair of khaki shorts on and was bare from the waist up. We had an all-dirt infield, and every day for a couple weeks he was out there raking up all the pebbles into a pile and going there with a wheelbarrow and shoveling them up, putting them in the wheelbarrow, taking them off the field, keeping the field as good as he could.

He came up to me and said, "You know what a hit-and-run is?"

I looked at him. "Well, no, no."

"Want to learn?"

I looked at my buddy and said, "Yeah, sure."

"See you at ten o'clock tomorrow morning."

So at ten o'clock the next day we're out there and here's this guy, a pretty good pitcher, and he's throwing balls over my head or over here and he says, "Hit it, hit it, hit it, hit it, hit it." You know, making me hit balls that are out of the strike zone, but of course, you have to make contact on a hit-and-run.

And he'd say, "Hit it to right field, hit it to right field," so we went on and on and on and on. This lasted for about a week, and I got pretty good.

And finally he disappeared. I went up to my manager one day and asked, "Whatever happened to that old guy who used to pitch batting practice to us, working with us on the hit-and-run?" and he said, "You mean Chief Bender?"

How do you like that? One of the great pitchers. One of Connie Mack's great, great money pitchers. Great money pitcher back in the teens, or, I guess, even before that. [Bender, a Hall of Famer, pitched from 1903 to 1917. He won 210 and lost 127. His 2.46 ERA is 23rd on the all-time list.] I never saw him again. He never told me who he was, just pitched batting practice. [Bender was 58 years old in 1942. He died in 1954.]

Actually, that helped me get to the big leagues, because I knew what a hit-and-run was, I knew how to execute, I could hit the ball the other way, and I could make contact. And I could bunt, I could do things like that. With the Yankees, I used to run Mize all the time, who couldn't walk across the field; but with first and third and less than two outs, especially one out, you don't want to hit into the double play, so you start the runner. If you hit the ball on the ground, you've got a run in and you've got a runner at second base.

# Chuck Diering

Nine years (1947–1952, 1954–1956)
Born: February 3, 1923  BR  TR  5'10"  165 lbs.
Positions: Outfield 631; 3B, 36; SS, 12
St. Louis Cardinals, New York Giants, Baltimore Orioles

| G | BA | AB | H | 2B | 3B | HR | R | RBI | BB | SO | SB | FA |
|---|-----|------|-----|----|----|----|-----|-----|-----|-----|----|------|
| 752 | .249 | 1648 | 411 | 76 | 14 | 14 | 217 | 141 | 237 | 250 | 16 | .984 |

*A*fter batting .305 and leading the Georgia-Florida
League with 102 runs scored in 1942, Diering spent
the next three years in the military. He played for the
Cardinals his first five years in the big leagues, then was
traded in December 1951 with Max Lanier to the Giants
for Eddie Stanky, who was named the Cardinals' manager.
In 1953 he batted .322 in 152 games for Minneapolis of
the American Association. He was voted the Baltimore
Orioles' Most Valuable Player in 1954. He was one of

*baseball's best defensive outfielders. In 1955–1956 he played 36 games at third base for Baltimore, committing only two errors (both in the same inning).*

# When Teams Protected Their Own

Harry Brecheen would buzz anybody; he was a mean pitcher, a tough competitor. We were playing against the Giants and Leo Durocher, and Johnny Mize was up. He was in a situation where a home run would have beat Harry. Harry pitched him inside. Mize just stands there and it hits him right between the shoulder blades just below the back of the neck. Mize runs to first base. That's it. The inning's over.

Brecheen comes up to hit the next inning. Leo Durocher calls time. He brings in Monte Kennedy, a hard, wild-throwing left-hander. And Leo probably told him, "Get him."

Kennedy threw a ball and hit Harry Brecheen in the right knee so hard I thought he broke his leg. Harry didn't say one word, dropped his bat, ran to first base, and finished out the inning. That poor guy couldn't walk for a week.

And this was the way things were. Everybody protected each other. Today you can't do that. That's why it's an altogether different ball game.

# *Advice from the Veterans*

Back in our days, we had about 600 guys in our farm club. You had to work your butt off whether you were hurt or not to hold your job. You had a one-year contract, you had to dicker with the management for contracts to get a raise, and the players themselves policed each other. I'll just give you a couple instances of what happened to me when I was a rookie.

I was out on the field and I had a broken shoelace in my shoe. Well, I didn't have a lot of money. And I had some old yellow shoelaces there in my locker, and I put them in my shoes, black shoes, and I came out on the field—black shoes, yellow shoelaces—and Slaughter saw that, and he said, "What are you doing with those yellow shoelaces?"

I said, "Well, I put them in; my other ones broke."

He said, "You get your butt back in there and put some black shoelaces in. You're in the major leagues now, you don't dress like that."

One day Marty Marion caught me at the hotel. I had one of these white t-shirts that you wear underneath your shirts. Well, I was wearing a white t-shirt under my sport coat. Marion stopped me and he said, "Chuck, you can't dress like that."

I said, "What do you mean, Marty?"

He said, "That shirt you got on."

I said, "It's new."

He said, "You can't wear a t-shirt around these hotels. You go out and buy yourself some shirts and be presentable. You're in the major leagues now."

So I mean, we had a lot of camaraderie that way. We had to win as a team, yet as an individual you were working for yourself. You had to. 'Cause you had to get your own contract. But when you got on that field, you were a 25-man team. You were out to do one thing, and that was to win the pennant and World Series and get that ring.

# Sonny Dixon

Four years (1953–1956)
Born: November 5, 1924   BB   TR   6'2 1/2"   205 lbs.
Position:  Pitcher
Washington Senators, Philadelphia Athletics,
Kansas City Athletics, New York Yankees

| G | W | L | PCT | ERA | GS | CG | SV | IP | H | BB | SO | BA | FA |
|---|---|---|-----|-----|-----|-----|-----|-----|-----|-----|-----|-----|-----|
| 102 | 11 | 18 | .379 | 4.17 | 12 | 4 | 9 | 263 | 296 | 63 | 94 | .180 | .989 |

*D*ixon pitched for nine minor league seasons—with a three-year interruption for military service—before joining the Washington Senators in 1953. From 1948 to 1952 his win totals were 11, 14, 14, 14, 19. In 1946 he led the Tri-State League with 19 wins for Charlotte. In 1954 he led the American League with 54 appearances while splitting time with Washington and Philadelphia. In 1955 he was traded with cash to the Yankees from Kansas City for Johnny Sain and Enos Slaughter.

## *Throwing the Ball Past Ted Williams*

Ted beat me in a ball game one night in Philadelphia in the 10th inning. Piersall was on first with two outs and I had three-and-two on him and he hit one on the fists, and you know they played him to right field—and he hit the ball and it hit the dirt at third base. One of them dying quails, I call them. It spun out back of third base. It hit the dirt, it didn't go nowhere, but everybody played him to pull and he ended up on second. Piersall scored.

Of course, I was mad. I walked out toward second base and he told me that I threw the ball by him.

I said, "If I can throw the ball by you I'll turn around and walk off, I ain't got no more to say."

## *Veeck's Broken Toe*

I guess you would say my greatest thrill was striking out three left-handed hitters in a row to save a ball game. We were in St. Louis, the old Sportsman's Park, the bases were loaded, we were leading 5-4 in the ninth inning. And the funny thing about it was that they had a right-hander and a left-hander, me and a left-hander, Al Sima, warming up in the bullpen. [Sima was 11-21 in his four-year career.] And I faced the three left-handers.

I struck out Dixie Upright, Dick Kokos, and Vic Wertz in that order.

By the way, Bill Veeck owned St. Louis. And when I struck out Wertz, Veeck jumped up—he was in the press box—he jumped up and kicked the chair with his good foot—you know he had an artificial leg. He kicked the chair with his good foot and broke his toe.

# A "Carolina" Strike

My first year up, Bill McGowan was umpiring a game in Boston. I had two strikes on Ted Williams and I threw a pitch I thought was right down the middle. McGowan called it a ball and I jumped about two feet in the air and hollered as loud as I could. I guess I was so excited. I don't know why Williams took it, I haven't the slightest idea. But I did know at that time I had done wrong, so I turned around and went straight to second base. I wouldn't even look at home plate because I knew McGowan was coming out.

Anyway, I stood out there a little bit and I sort of turned around and he was going back behind the plate. So I finally got Williams out somehow.

Usually, the home plate umpire goes down toward first base after the inning's over, but our dugout faced third base. So McGowan started down toward third base when I was coming across the line, and I knew he was going to make me walk right in front of him, the way he was going. So I didn't even look. I had my head down. Of course, I was looking out of the corner of my eye, and when I stepped right in front of him, he said, "It might have been a strike in Carolina, but that so-and-so was not a strike up here."

And I just kept on walking because I knew if I said one word to him, I'd have been out of the ball game.

# Bobby Doerr

14 years (1937–1944, 1946–1951)
Born: April 7, 1918   BR   TR   5'11"   175 lbs.
Position: Second Base
Boston Red Sox

| G | BA | AB | H | 2B | 3B | HR | R | RBI | BB | SO | SB | FA |
|---|----|----|----|----|----|----|----|-----|----|----|----|----|
| 1865 | .288 | 7093 | 2042 | 381 | 89 | 223 | 1094 | 1247 | 809 | 608 | 54 | .980 |

*A* nine-time All-Star, Doerr was elected to the Hall of Fame in 1986. He was one of baseball's finest defensive second basemen. In his 13 full seasons with the Red Sox, he never batted under .270, and he hit at least 21 doubles each season. He hit 12 or more home runs in each of his last 12 seasons, twice hitting highs of 27. Six times he drove in more than 100 runs, with a career-high 120 in 1950. His career total of 1,247 RBI is 79th on the all-time list. Doerr hit over .300 three times, with a high of .325 in 1944, when he led the league with a .528 slug-

*ging percentage. He had a league-leading 11 triples in 1950. A durable player, he averaged 142 games a year over a 12-year stretch. He played four years of minor league ball before joining the Red Sox in 1937. In his only World Series, a loss to the Cardinals in 1946, he batted .409 in 22 at-bats, with a double and a home run.*

# Sing a Song

Joe Cronin was an outstanding manager. Playing alongside him helped me so much as a young kid. He kept talking to me about different things. He told me what I might look for from the pitchers I was going to face. He talked to me about how to position in the field. If I hadn't played alongside him, I would have had to learn some of those things the hard way.

Sometimes I'd come out all keyed up because I wasn't hitting or something, and he'd say, "Oh, relax. Sing a song." I don't know how many times he told me that. I got to feeling, "If he's not worried about what I'm doing, why should I be uptight about it?" I look back on it as one of the nice things he did to help me.

# Ted's Tryout

I joined the Hollywood team in the Coast League in 1934 and played the rest of that season, and then all

*Bobby Doerr*

of '35. In 1936 they moved their franchise to San Diego, and that's where I got to see Ted Williams come in for a tryout in June that year. He was just out of high school and just came out for a tryout. We were standing by the batting cage and this big skinny kid was standing right in front of me. Nobody knew who he was—it was the first time we'd ever seen him. Our manager, Frank Shellenback, was pitching batting practice, and he said, "Let the kid get in and hit a few," and of course all the old players were grumbling about Ted going to take up their time in batting practice. When he got in and hit—I think he hit about seven or eight balls, line drives, a couple of them out of the ballpark, and had that great swing—everybody started changing their tune a little bit. Who's this kid? So I was always kind of proud to know that I got to see Ted come in for that tryout and then play the rest of my career with him.

He was one of those unusual guys, one of those one-in-a-lifetime guys. Everything he did was done to perfection. He wanted to be good, and he was good. He was so much sharper than everybody else, as far as using percentages to make him a better hitter. And when you had a guy like Ted Williams on your ball club, why, I think it made everybody just a little more conscious of their hitting.

# Jim Dyck

Six years (1951–1956)

Born: February 3, 1922  BR  TR  6'2"  200 lbs.

Positions: Outfield, 157;  3B, 147; 1B, 1

St. Louis Browns, Cleveland Indians, Baltimore Orioles,

Cincinnati Reds

| G | BA | AB | H | 2B | 3B | HR | R | RBI | BB | SO | SB | FA |
|---|----|----|----|----|----|----|----|-----|----|----|----|----|
| 330 | .246. | 983 | 242 | 52 | 5 | 26 | 139 | 140 | 131 | 140 | 4 | .961 |

*D*yck was named to The Sporting News Major League All-Rookie team in 1952 at the age of 30, when he hit .269 with 15 home runs as a third baseman-outfielder with the Browns. His career was interrupted for three years for military service. Still, in the minor leagues he was an All-Star at every level in the Yankee organization: D, C, B, A, AA, and in three different AAA leagues. He helped preserve Bobo Holloman's 1953 no-hitter (in Holloman's first big-league start) with a leaping catch against the left-field wall. Dyck led the Western Associa-

*tion in 1946 in RBI (104) and batting (.364). In 1951 he led the Texas League in RBI with 127. In 1955 he hit .378 in 78 games for Indianapolis in the American Association and .279 in 61 games for the Baltimore Orioles.*

## Satch's Control

Satchel Paige was unbelievable with his control. We brought Satch in relief to pitch to one hitter, like with the bases loaded with two outs, and we had to get the hitter out or they were either going to tie or win the game. The guy hit a one-hopper right back to Satch. He fielded the ball, and he never even glanced toward first. He threw it under his left arm and he threw a perfect strike to the first baseman.

When he threw the ball, he turned and started walking to the dugout, never looked to see where it went, and of course he threw it right, a perfect throw, without looking.

I followed him from third base into the dugout. Hornsby was on the top step and he said, "That just cost you five hundred dollars. You ever do that again and I'll see that you never play for me again."

And Satch never even slowed down. He just walked on by, and I walked up the runway behind him, and I could hear Satch saying, "That crazy old man, what'd he think, they's going to move first base?  It's been there ever since I've played."

# *Jimmy Dykes*

I played for Jimmy Dykes, and we both had some fun with the similarity of our names. We'd be on road trips and he'd never take a phone call. They'd page for "Jimmy Dykes, Jimmy Dykes." He'd find me sitting over there, and he'd point at me and tell me to take the call. I'd go to the phone, and maybe it would be a newspaper reporter.

He'd say, "Jimmy Dykes?"

I'd say, "Yeah."

He'd say, "Who's pitching tomorrow?"

I'd say, "Well, hang on a minute." I'd go over to Jimmy, and I'd say, "Jimmy, they want to know who's pitching."

He'd say, "Tell them."

I'd say, "Who is it?"

He'd say, "Well, pick one."

So I'd go back and say, "So-and-so's pitching." Stuff like that.

Jimmy came down for breakfast in the morning and said, "Jimmy, come here." I walked over and he said, "Oh, you know what happened last night?"

"What?"

He said, "About 12:30 at night the phone rang, and here's this really sweet-talking gal on the phone, and she said, 'Jimmy, can I come up?' and I said, 'Yeah, come up, but don't turn the lights on when you get in the room.' She said, 'Okay, I'll be right up.' Boy, did I have a nice night."

I loved Jimmy. Our mail was a joke. He'd get my mail and I'd get his mail all the time. Then he wound up as a coach over at Cincinnati, and I wound up with Cincinnati, too. Baltimore traded me over there supposedly as a right-handed pinch hitter when Tebbetts was managing. I walked in the clubhouse and the first guy I see is Jimmy Dykes. He looked at me and said, "Oh, man, not you again."

He was a neat guy.

# *Two Homers in One Inning*

We were playing in Shreveport when I was with San Antonio in the Texas League, and I came up twice in the seventh inning and homered both times. I thought, "This is unusual to hit two home runs in one inning. It must have at least tied a record."

Well, it didn't. The record for home runs in one inning was three. And it was set in the Texas League by a player in Waco, Texas. They had a little bitty bandbox ballpark, and the home runs used to just jump out of there, I guess, and some guy hit three in one inning. So I didn't even tie a record. That was kind of a shock to me. [In 1930, Gene Rye, a 5'6", 165-pound left-handed-hitting outfielder for Waco, accomplished the feat against Beaumont. He led off the eighth inning of the first night game ever broadcast in the Texas

League with a home run over the right-field fence. His second time up he hit a three-run homer over the right-field fence. His third time up, he hit a grand slam over the center-field fence. Waco scored 18 runs in the inning and won 20-7. In his brief big-league career, in 1931, Rye went 7-for-39, all singles.]

# *Pitching on the Black*

Allie Reynolds, I swear, he pitched me a whole season and never used more than the black part of the plate on the outside. I liked to pull the ball and I'd try to pull off him and he would force me to go the other way. He just would never make a mistake. Allie was the kind of guy, you would go up maybe your first time at bat on a given day, and you'd think, boy, he ain't throwing all that hard. That curveball wasn't all that much.

Then you'd come up in the eighth or ninth in the clutch and it was like a different pitcher. He coasted, and he saved his stuff for when he needed it. Boy, then he'd just explode a fastball on you, when you hadn't seen one anywhere near that speed all day. His curveball would get sharper all of a sudden. He'd just reach back and get it when he needed it. He was really tough.

# *Rain Dance*

We had very few days off and always played a doubleheader on Sundays and holidays. We loved to play, but it was a long season. The few days off we got were welcome breaks.

We all became quite good as weather forecasters. Sometimes we'd even do rain dances, and shout, "Come on, Jupe!" That was our way of asking Jupiter for rain.

Sometimes the dances worked.

# *Mantle's Brainstorm*

This was in Sportsman's Park, St. Louis. Browns vs. Yanks. I was playing third base, top of the ninth, two outs, nobody on base, Browns ahead by one.

With two strikes on Mickey, I moved back onto the left-field grass. My teammates and I were all hoping he wouldn't hit one out.

Mickey bunted the next pitch foul and the game was over!

We couldn't believe what happened and just stood in our positions with our mouths hanging open.

I understand Casey Stengel informed Mickey that from now on he would do the thinking and Mick should just stick to playing!

# *Unexpected Help*

I had played a long minor league career by the time I got to the big leagues. In my first game, when I took my position at third base and I got ready to play the first hitter, a voice behind me said, "About two steps to your right, kid."

I moved over two steps to my right, and the batter hit a ground ball right at me. I didn't turn around, I just said, "Thanks a lot, ump."

I went to play the next hitter, and he said, "You'd better get over in the hole a bit." So I moved a little bit to my left, and he just steered me around the whole ball game. Finally, I said to him, "Geez, this is nice when you've got an umpire behind you telling you where to play. Why are you doing that?"

He said, "We've got the word on you. We'll take care of you."

That was fun.

# Ferris Fain

Nine years (1947–1955)
Born: May 29, 1921   BL   TL   5'11"   180 lbs.
Position: First Base
Philadelphia Athletics, Chicago White Sox, Detroit Tigers,
Cleveland Indians

| G | BA | AB | H | 2B | 3B | HR | R | RBI | BB | SO | SB | FA |
|---|---|---|---|---|---|---|---|---|---|---|---|---|
| 1151 | .290 | 3930 | 1139 | 213 | 30 | 48 | 595 | 570 | 904 | 261 | 46 | .987 |

*A* *five-time All-Star, Fain led the American League in batting twice, with a .344 mark in 1951 and .327 in 1952. His 43 doubles led the league in 1952. He had over 100 walks five times in his career and had a career on-base percentage of .425. A great contact hitter, for his career he struck out only once per 15 at-bats. Perhaps the league's best-fielding first baseman, he led the league in assists four times and set a major league record for double plays (194 in 1949). The Athletics got Joe DeMaestri, Ed*

*McGhee, and Eddie Robinson in the 1953 trade that sent*
*Fain to the White Sox. In 1954 he was involved in a trade*
*with Detroit for Walt Dropo, Ted Gray, and Bob Nieman.*
*In a five-year career with San Francisco in the Pacific*
*Coast League (interrupted for three years of military*
*service), he twice hit over .300 and led the league in 1941*
*with 122 runs scored and in 1946 with 117 runs scored*
*and 112 RBI.*

# *How to Win a Batting Title*

I t was actually blisters that turned my career around.
Going to spring training in 1951 I'd never hit .300
in the big leagues. But I got bad blisters on my hands.

Rather than lose my turn in the batting cage, I
choked up on the bat like you would do in pepper,
3-4 inches, and just tried making contact with the
ball. All of a sudden, I started hitting line drives
wherever I wanted to. I thought, "What the heck?
What happened?" All of a sudden I had become a
credible hitter.

It was sheer luck, how it came about, but now I
had complete control of the bat; the bat didn't control
me. I could put the bat just where I wanted to, not like
the big hitters who hold it on the end and can't get any
consistency. Consistency is the name of the game; it
turned my career around. I thought, "Well, as long as
this is working, I'll stay with it." I hit .344 that year
and led the league. [Fain also led the league in 1952

*Ferris Fain*

with a .327 average and hit a league-leading 43 doubles.]

## *Piersall on the Bases*

When I was at first base, I chatted with everybody. Ted Williams—you couldn't shut him up; he always wanted to talk. Joe DiMaggio—I played with him in the service, the greatest all-around player I've ever seen. He did everything so gracefully, did it all in stride. But he didn't say much. He was cordial at first base, but he wouldn't carry on a conversation. Jimmy Piersall—he'd start singing at first base, three words from one song, a phrase from another that didn't match—none of it made sense. "Holy cow!" I'd think. "Let's get this guy to second; he's making me nervous!"

## *True Enjoyment*

I'm sure there was more true enjoyment in playing baseball in the '50s. We didn't have the money to worry about. We didn't have free agency that makes players look ahead two or three years and wonder where they will be playing and worrying about injuries that might keep them from big money. For me, the competition was everything. I just enjoyed the thrill of it. I was getting paid to do something I loved to do. If I had a good day, that's wonderful; if I didn't, I wasn't going to jump off the bridge. I loved getting out in the afternoon, getting out on the freshly cut lawn. Every day was a different game.

# Making Him Squirm

I charged the mound once, but fortunately, the umpire grabbed me by my shirt and held me back. I'm glad he did. I had forgotten just how big that pitcher was. Getting a pitch thrown under your chin is a compliment. It tells you that you're making this guy squirm a bit. It's only when the guy is trying to kill you, throwing fastballs intentionally at your head, that there's any justification for charging the mound. Some of the players today charge the pitcher after getting thrown at by a dinky little spinning curveball. That's no cause for charging the mound.

# Don Ferrarese

Eight years (1955–1962)
Born: June 19, 1929   BR   TL   5'9"   170 lbs.
Position: Pitcher
Baltimore Orioles, Cleveland Indians, Chicago White Sox,
Philadelphia Phillies, St. Louis Cardinals

| G | W | L | PCT | ERA | GS | CG | SV | IP | H | BB | SO | BA | FA |
|---|---|---|-----|-----|-----|-----|-----|------|-----|-----|-----|------|------|
| 183 | 19 | 36 | .345 | 4.00 | 50 | 12 | 5 | 506.2 | 244 | 295 | 350 | .156 | .952 |

*With a great fastball and one of baseball's best curveballs, Ferrarese was hampered early in his career by control problems and later by arm trouble. He walked 567 batters in his first 522 professional innings, while striking out 502. He walked just five per nine innings in the major leagues. In 1954 he won 18 games and batted .300 for Oakland in the Pacific Coast League. In 1955, for San Antonio in the Texas League, he walked*

*47 in 99 innings, going 9-0 with a 1.48 ERA. In his first big-league start, he struck out 13 men, but lost to Cleveland 2-1. On the same day that Carl Erskine pitched a no-hitter against the Giants in 1956, Don lost a no-hitter against the Yankees in the ninth inning on an infield hit by Andy Carey, but won the game 1-0 on Don's RBI off Bob Turley. In a 1959 game, he hit three consecutive doubles off Dick Donovan.*

## But I Got Them Out!

My first game was in relief on opening day of 1955 in Washington. My first hitter was Mickey Vernon. I had the bases loaded, and he popped up. And that got me one out. Runnels—Pete Runnels—was the second hitter, and I got him out somehow.

So here I am, I've got opening day in Washington, the president's there, and I get the two outs, and they take me out of the ball game. I said, "What did I do wrong?" Of course, I wasn't used to being taken out in the minors, this right-handed-left-handed thing, you know what I mean? And I was devastated.

And, of course, the old-timers understood. Harry Dorish, I remember in particular, got me aside. He said, "No, this is the way we do it. You didn't do anything wrong. We just keep switching—you know." But I didn't know about that.

# *Billy Martin*

I n the '40s, Billy went to Berkeley High School, and I went to a little school that produced Norm Van Brocklin, the great quarterback, called Acalenes High School. Billy was a senior and I was a junior, and I was a big phenom in the Bay area. So my coach and their coach were in different leagues and said, "Well, let's see what this little guy can do against a bigger school," 'cause we had about a thousand kids and they had about 5,000 kids, and Billy was the big star.

So I'm in the seventh inning and I've got a no-hitter and I'm beating them 1-0, and Billy's in the on-deck circle and he's taunting me as I'm taking my warm-ups. "I'm going to beat you single-handedly, you little son of a gun. I'll beat you—."

So he gets a bloop single over second base, gets on first base, steals second, taunting me the whole way. Gets on second, steals third. Gets on third, and he steals home, but as he's almost to home plate, the batter fouled the ball off. That would have tied the game. Billy had to go back to third base, and I subsequently got the guy out somehow, and we won the game 1-0.

About 10 years later, in 1956, we became team-mates in Cleveland. In about the sixth, seventh inning, I got taken out of a game. Finally, Billy gets out of the game and he comes in while I'm taking a shower. I've got soap suds all over my head and I can't see, but I feel some warm water on my leg. I get the soap suds out of my eyes, and I said, "What the heck are you doing?"

He said, "I'm taking a leak on you. You son of a gun, if that guy hadn't have fouled the ball off back in 1946, I'd have beat you single-handedly."

# *Setting Up Lollar*

I tied a record for pitchers by hitting three consecutive doubles in a game.

Sherman Lollar was the catcher. Dick Donovan was the pitcher. First time up, I hit a double, drove in a run, in Comiskey. Second time I come up, I hit another double. Third time I came up, Lollar said, "Lefty, you're hitting the ball too good, we're going to have to knock you on your butt."

So here comes a fastball right at my head. I went down, brushed myself off.

Lollar laughed.

I said, "Sherm, all you've gotta to do is throw me curveballs. I can't hit curves."

So here comes a big curve I knew was coming, and I almost hit it out of the park. Drove in the second run. I won the game 3-0.

Anyhow, Lollar's yelling at me as I'm rounding the base, "You little jerk, you set me up for that thing!" It's sort of neat. Because pitchers don't get to brag about their hitting much.

# A Humbling Moment

My first year up, I'd just struck out 13 and beat the Yankees. Then we go into Boston and I'm the starting pitcher in Fenway. Ted Williams was running to left field, and he made a comment to me. He said, "You're the kid with the good curveball, I hear, huh?" And that was it. Ted Williams spoke to me.

I was with the Orioles at the time. Our second baseman, Billy Gardner, was playing short right field. We had no third baseman, no shortstop, and no left fielder. So Ted stands up there, and I throw him a curveball, and he stood there motionless. Strike one. Second one, I threw a curve ball over the plate. Motionless again. So I said to myself, "Man, I can get this guy."

Well, the third one I threw, he hit so hard that the force of the ball knocked Billy Gardner over in short right field. Billy caught a snow cone. As Ted rounded first base, he spat into the air and said, "Kid, you can take your curveball and shove it."

It was a very humbling experience. And the thing that impressed me about him was the fact that when he swung at a ball, he hit it. And when he took a ball, there was no lunging, no movement at all. It was awesome.

And the umpires would never call him out on a third strike. They'd only call a third strike on Ted Williams if he dropped the bat and walked away;

otherwise, they'd never call him out. So you had to throw the ball right down the middle to him.

But he was a great hitter.

# Tom Ferrick

Nine years  (1941–1942, 1946–1952)
Born: January 6, 1915   BR   TR   6'2 1/2"   220 lbs.
Position:  Pitcher
Philadelphia Athletics, Cleveland Indians, St. Louis Browns,
Washington Senators, New York Yankees

| G | W | L | PCT | ERA | GS | CG | SV | IP | H | BB | SO | BA | FA |
|---|---|---|-----|-----|----|----|----|----|---|----|----|----|----|
| 323 | 40 | 40 | .500 | 3.47 | 74 | 56 | 6 | 74 | 654 | 227 | 245 | .184 | .953 |

*F*errick signed in 1936 and was 26 years old when he
joined Connie Mack's Athletics in 1941. He started
four games among his 36 appearances and pitched one
shutout, winning eight and losing 10. He started only
three more games during the next eight seasons. He spent
three years in the Navy and returned to go 4-1 in 1946.
He came to the Yankees on June 15, 1950, in an eight-
player trade with the Browns and played a key role in

*their pennant and World Series wins. He went 8-4 in
relief with nine saves in 30 relief appearances during the
rest of the season. He won Game 3 of the World Series in
relief of Lopat. On June 15, 1951, he went to Washington
with Fred Sanford and Bob Porterfield for Bob Kuzava.
Ferrick was a pitching coach in the big leagues for 12 years
and then became a longtime scout.*

## Nobody Dragged a Wagon

Was it easier to pitch for the Yankees than for
some other teams? Well, I'll put it this way: you
didn't need any urging, because with the Yankees, when
you walked into the ballpark in a Yankee uniform, you
knew you were gonna win, in any way, shape, or form.
The attitude that they had was great. Nobody dragged a
wagon over there.

*Tom Ferrick*

# *DiMaggio, the Catalyst*

DiMaggio was the catalyst for that whole Yankee ball club. He was a living example; he didn't have to tell you anything. We were playing a doubleheader in Washington in 1950, and it was always hot there. Joe D was ailing; he had a bad ankle. He played the first game in center field, and Casey decided to play him at first base in the second game so he wouldn't have to do too much, and I came in to relieve late in the game.

Somebody hit a swinging bunt down the first-base line. I was kind of indecisive about it. I fielded it and threw the ball into the runner just as Joe got to the bag. He could have got killed. I thought to myself, "Boy, if I put Joe out of action, they'll send me out to Podunk." But he survived. After the game, he told Stengel, "That's the last time I'm playing first base." He went back to the outfield. [In his 13-year career, he played 1,721 games in the outfield, one game at first base.]

Joe was a great model. He did everything to perfection. He exerted himself. When he left home plate on a base hit in the gap, he knew just what base he was going to end up at. Even with his bone spur on his heel, he forced himself to get to that point. He led by example, and he just had to give some of the guys a look once in awhile, that were dragging the wagon. They got the message.

# *Learning a Lesson*

I was a right-handed pitcher, and I had a flexible delivery, three-quarters, and I could throw side-armed. Some right-handed hitters didn't like side-armed pitching—they'd give ground—and I found out quickly who they were. When I was with the Athletics my rookie year [in 1941], there was an old pitcher on the A's by the name of Johnny Babich [Ferrick was 26, Babich was 28]. Babich had been in the Yankee organization. He kind of adopted me, helped me out. The Yankees came into Philadelphia for a series and Babich said to me, "Make sure you sidearm DiMaggio. He don't like it, he's not as effective." So the first time I pitched against him, I sidearmed him twice. He took one pitch and he swung at the second one and missed it. And then, finally, I got one inside and he hit it off the wall. That was the last time I did that. You learn a lesson.

# Bob Friend

16 years (1951–1966)
Born: November 24, 1930   BR   TR   6'   190 lbs.
Position: Pitcher
Pittsburgh Pirates, New York Yankees, New York Mets

| G | W | L | PCT | ERA | GS | CG | SV | IP | H | BB | SO | BA | FA |
|---|---|---|-----|-----|----|----|----|-----|---|----|----|----|----|
| 602 | 197 | 230 | .461 | 3.58 | 497 | 163 | 113 | 61137 | 228 | 941 | 734 | .121 | .969 |

*A three-time All-Star, Friend averaged over 15 wins a season for the Pirates from 1955 to 1964, winning at least 13 in nine of those 10 seasons. One of baseball's most durable pitchers, he pitched at least 200 innings in 11 straight seasons. He pitched 36 shutouts, including a league-leading five in 1962. In 1955 he led the NL with a 2.83 ERA, the first pitcher ever to accomplish the feat pitching for a last-place team. In 1958 he tied Spahn in wins with 22. In 1960 he helped lead the Pirates to a* pennant with 18 wins, including seven in the final two months of the season. He was the winning pitcher in the 1956 and 1960 All-Star Games. In the 1956 he recorded his last three outs of the game by striking out three left-handed batters in succession—Mantle, Berra, and Ted Williams. Friend graduated from Purdue University. The Pirates' player representative, he went on to a successful career in local politics in Pittsburgh after his playing days ended.

## Coming Special Delivery

Branch Rickey was general manager at Pittsburgh. I was playing for the minimum salary, five thousand dollars, in 1951 and '52. I wanted a thousand-dollar raise and he orchestrated this thing where I flew in from Indiana and went out to his house. Branch Jr. was there.

Branch mentioned to Junior, "Have the boys signed their contracts yet?" and the Twig said, "No, they haven't. We've just got one under contract."

Then Senior said, "That's good, we don't need them. We finished in last place, we can finish last without them." And then he said, "Bob, I assume you're one of the guys that signed your contract."

I said, "Well, I think I just put it in the mail yesterday."

He had a way of really getting to you, but he was a great person and it was quite a thrill being associated with him for four or five years.

# *Haddix's Perfect Game*

I was Harvey Haddix's roommate when he pitched that perfect game in Milwaukee [12 perfect innings; he lost the game in the 13th]. Just an outstanding night. Well, everybody was in shock that we didn't win the game, but also, it was amazing—everybody knew by the fifth inning he had a no-hitter, but a lot of us didn't realize that it was a perfect game until later on. I didn't realize it was a perfect game until after the game. I knew he had a no-hitter, you know. But it wasn't any fluke. His pitches were solid, in a good spot, and they were all strong—a good slider, a hard fastball, and a good change of pace. Everything was working.

# Ned Garver

14 years (1948–1961)
Born: December 25, 1925  BR  TR  5'10 1/5"  180 lbs.
Position: Pitcher
St. Louis Browns, Detroit Tigers, Kansas City Athletics,
Los Angeles Angels

| G | W | L | PCT | ERA | GS | CG | SV | IP | H | BB | SO | BA | FA |
|---|---|---|-----|-----|----|----|----|-----|----|----|----|----|----|
| 402 | 129 | 157 | .451 | 3.73 | 330 | 153 | 12 | 2477.1 | 471 | 881 | 881 | .218 | .961 |

*Garver pitched 18 big-league shutouts. He won 20 games for the Browns in 1951, hitting .305. The only 20th-century pitcher to win 20 games for a team that lost 100, Garver saw one of his seven big-league home runs help him win his 20th game. He was on the All-Star team in 1951. His $25,000 contract in 1952 made him the highest-paid Brown in history. He led the American League in complete games in 1950 and 1951. He won 10 or more games eight times, all with second-division teams.*

# *That Dad-Blamed Railroad Car*

In the Texas League we played where we didn't have air-conditioned railroad cars to ride in. You'd ride in a dad-blamed railroad car that's been sitting out there in the yards all day in the sun of over a hundred degrees. Then you'd get to a hotel, and sometimes they weren't air-conditioned either. We went into Shreveport, the railroad went right by there, and you had to have the window open because it wasn't air-conditioned, and the dad-blamed soot from the coal-burning engines would have you all speckled in the morning.

# *No One Was Better*

Satchel Paige was the greatest pitcher ever, no one even close. He had great stuff, created pitches like the hesitation pitch. Satchel knew more about attacking a hitter from the pitcher's mound than anyone I ever saw. No one close.

I asked Charlie Gehringer, "How good was Satchel when you toured with Bob Feller?"

Charlie said, "I never hit against anyone better."

Tommy Bridges taught me some things. Harry Kimberland there at Toledo taught me some things. A guy by the name of Moose Markem taught me some things about getting behind the hitter and pitching from behind, and it was a learning experience.

But Satchel Paige knew more about getting hitters out, about pitching in each situation, than anybody who ever drew a breath. Satchel Paige pitched more innings, he pitched in more games, he pitched like 28 years in a row, winter and summer. He'd been wherever there was as far as a pitcher. Oh, man, I loved that guy, and I loved to talk to him. He was something else, boy. I'm so glad I got to know that sucker.

We were playing an exhibition game in York, Pennsylvania, a farm club of ours. They brought Satch in to pitch the last inning. He stalled away out there like he didn't have good control. He walked the first three batters. He scraped around at the mound. He took the dad-blamed rosin bag and threw it down in disgust, just like he was all upset, and the people were hollering like as if they thought, "Boy, oh boy, we're going to do something against Satchel Paige, he's got the bases loaded . . ." He threw nine pitches and he struck out the next three guys. Now, that's the God's truth. That's the way it went. He enjoyed that type of thing. If we had a big lead with nothing on the line, he would create something that would entertain. He was a colorful, wonderful pitcher. Too bad he couldn't have been in the major leagues as long as he deserved to be.

*Ned Garver*

# The 20th Win

I remember a lot about that 20th win. I remember that before the game started, the Globetrotters played basketball there on a court that they set up behind third base. It was Goose Tatum and Marcus Haynes and those guys. I wanted to play because I'd played a lot of basketball. But I couldn't do that because I was pitching.

Then the game started. I got hit pretty good, but the game was tied in about the fifth inning and I hit a ball over the left-field fence in the stands and it put us ahead and it kept us there. I hit it off Randy Gumpert, a Chicago White Sox pitcher. I hit that son of a biscuit over the Sealy Mattress sign in left-center field. Boy! Yep, I won't forget that. I mean, I'll have Alzheimer's pretty bad before I forget that.

# Joe Ginsberg

13 years (1948, 1950–1954, 1956–1962)
Born: October 11, 1926  BL  TR  5'11"  180 lbs.
Position: Catcher
Detroit Tigers, Cleveland Indians, Kansas City Athletics,
Baltimore Orioles, Chicago White Sox, Boston Red Sox,
New York Mets

| G | BA | AB | H | 2B | 3B | HR | R | RBI | BB | SO | SB | FA |
|-----|------|------|-----|----|----|----|-----|-----|-----|-----|----|------|
| 695 | .241 | 1716 | 414 | 59 | 8 | 20 | 168 | 182 | 226 | 125 | 7 | .983 |

*Ginsberg made his major league debut for Detroit in 1948 and batted .361 in 11 games. Twice he played more than 100 games for Detroit, batting .260 in 102 games in 1951 and .221 in 113 games in 1952. He hit 14 of his 20 career home runs in those two seasons. He caught a Virgil Trucks no-hitter (1-0) in 1952. He was one of the players involved in a trade for Ray Boone in 1953. He was the starting catcher in the first game the*

*Mets ever played in the Polo Grounds. He twice hit over .300 in the minors: .326 for Williamsport in 1947 and .336 for Toledo in 1950.*

## Casey Stengel with the Mets

It was a hot day in New York—it had to be a hundred degrees—and Casey was managing the Mets and he fell asleep in the dugout. He was sleeping along, and all of a sudden he heard the crack of the bat. It woke him up and he started applauding and said, "Well fellas, that's the way to go, hitting the ball—"

And we had to tell him, "Casey, that's not us, that's the other team running the bases."

But Casey was about 75 years old then and naturally, things happen like that when you get to be 75, I guess. But he was good for a laugh every time. He'd be with those sportswriters, and he'd drink with them all night if they wanted to, and he would tell them stories until the wee hours. Casey was something else.

## Shrewd Casey Stengel

Back when they had elevator operators in the hotel, Casey told us his rules on curfew: "Fellas, there's a two o'clock curfew. I want everybody in their rooms and sleeping by two o'clock after a night game." Some of the guys were a little older, and at two o'clock weren't ready to go to bed.

Now we came home to the hotel and got on the elevator, and the elevator person had a baseball, and he said, "Fellows, would you sign this for me?" A lot of us that got in a little later, we signed the darn ball.

The next morning at the ballpark, Casey said, "Okay, you, you, you, and you come into my office."

We all came into his office, and he said, "You guys didn't make curfew."

We said, "How do you know that, Case?"

He said, "You see this baseball?  I gave it to the elevator operator and told him to get every one of you to sign after two o'clock in the morning."

So that's how he found out we were late.

## Victory Party

When I was with the Mets, we lost our first nine games in 1962. When the next game was rained out, Stengel called everyone into the clubhouse for a big spread of food and drink.

He said, "This is a victory party. No one will beat us today."

# *Catching an Art Houtteman One-Hitter*

I caught Art Houtteman's one-hitter against Cleveland. As a matter of fact, we had two outs in the ninth inning. And doggone, his name was Suitcase Simpson, I'll never forget it. We had gotten him out twice on a certain pitch, and I called that certain pitch again. To this day, Art and I argue about it.

I tell him, "If you'd have listened to me, I'd have had you in the Hall of Fame," but no, he wanted to throw his own pitch. I called a curveball, he shook me off. I called a curveball again, he shook me off. He threw a fastball and Simpson hit a line drive between short and third and broke up his no-hitter.

And I really felt bad about it. So did Art, but we wound up beating Cleveland by a dozen or so runs, so it didn't mean a heck of a lot except that Art lost his no-hitter.

We're both Detroit boys, and we've known each other an awfully long time, and I never let him forget that pitch. Whenever I see him, the first thing I say is, "You want to shake me off again?"

# Elephant Glove

Hoyt Wilhelm was the toughest pitcher to catch. He put a lot of catchers in the Hall of Shame. Paul Richards created the "Elephant Glove" to catch Wilhelm with. It was so big that catchers had a hard time getting the ball out of the glove to throw out baserunners. The ball looked like a butterfly coming up to the plate around 50-55 miles per hour. It was especially tough to catch and hit with the wind blowing out.

# Red Jones

Red Jones was probably the funniest man umpiring behind the plate you ever heard in your life. He really couldn't see very well, and he knew it, but he wouldn't wear glasses, because at that time, if you wore glasses, the fans would just get all over you. Whenever he missed a pitch, he always claimed the catcher jumped up and blocked his vision. One time the count was 1-and-1—the pitch seemed to me that it was right down the middle—and the guy was running. I jumped up and threw the ball to second base, and all Red said was, "Two!"

I turned around and said, "Two, Red? Two what?"

He said, "Where was it?"

I said, "It was right down the middle."

He said, "Two strikes!" He just didn't know where the ball was.

# Randy Gumpert

10 years (1938–1938, 1946–1952)
Born: January 23, 1918  BR  TR  6'3"  185 lbs.
Position: Pitcher
Philadelphia Athletics, New York Yankees, Chicago White Sox,
Boston Red Sox, Washington Senators

| G | W | L | PCT | ERA | GS | CG | SV | IP | H | BB | SO | BA | FA |
|---|---|---|-----|-----|-----|-----|-----|-----|-----|-----|-----|-----|-----|
| 261 | 51 | 59 | .464 | 4.17 | 113 | 47 | 7 | 1052.2 | 1099 | 346 | 352 | .182 | .951 |

*A*n All-Star in 1951 with the White Sox, Gumpert
had his best season with the Yankees in 1946 (11-3
with a 2.31 ERA). In 1949 he completed 18 of his 32
starts with the White Sox and pitched three of his six
career shutouts. He pitched 36 games for the Athletics
between 1936 and 1938, but did not get back to the
major leagues until 1946 (he spent '43, '44, and '45 in
military service). Before signing with the Athletics in

*1936, he pitched two years of batting practice for the A's in Shibe Park.*

## The Four-Base Walk

Paul Richards was the best manager I played for. He was a fellow like Tony LaRussa. No-nonsense and very dedicated to the game. I liked to play for Paul. There's a play involving Paul Richards that probably nobody alive today knows about. When he got the White Sox job in 1951, we trained in California. The first day, I walked over to Paul and said, "Paul, do you remember that day in Philadelphia back in 1935?"

He said, "You know, I didn't think anybody was around that would remember that anymore."

I said, "Yes, I happened to be at the ball game. I had pitched batting practice that day."

He said, "Well, don't let the word get out."

Well, what happened, he was a redneck southerner from Waxahachie, Texas, and he was catching this particular day against Detroit. Charlie Gehringer was the hitter. Gehringer gets a base on balls, ball four, and Richards thought it should have been called a strike for strike three. So he turns around, has the ball in his hand and he has his mask off, and he's jawing with the umpire. Gehringer goes to first base. Everybody's screaming at Richards to give the ball back to the pitcher. Gehringer sees what happens so he runs down to second base. He runs to third base and he runs home. He scores on a base on balls without any intervening play.

I don't think it ever happened any time before then, and about two days later, Richards wound up in Atlanta. Mr. Mack had no patience with him on that. [Richards, as a 26-year-old catcher, played 85 games for the Athletics in 1935. He didn't play in the big leagues again until 1943, with Detroit.]

That's a true story, and I'm probably the only one left anymore who saw that thing. But I didn't know it was Gehringer until Richards told me. He said, "Yes, Charlie Gehringer was the hitter."

# Dick Hall

16 years  (1955–1957, 1959–1971)
Born: September 27, 1930  BR  TR  6'6"  200 lbs.
Position: Pitcher  (OF, 119; 2B, 7; 3B, 5; 1B, 1)
Pittsburgh Pirates, Kansas City Athletics, Baltimore Orioles,
Philadelphia Phillies

| G | W | L | PCT | ERA | GS | CG | SV | IP | H | BB | SO | BA | FA |
|---|---|---|---|---|---|---|---|---|---|---|---|---|---|
| 495 | 93 | 75 | .554 | 3.32 | 74 | 20 | 68 | 1259 | 1152 | 236 | 741 | .210 | .976 |

*H*all *pitched for four pennant-winning teams in
Baltimore and pitched in the 1969, 1970, and
1971 World Series. Signed as an outfielder with Pittsburgh, he played three minor league seasons as an outfielder. In his first year of pitching, he led the Western
League with a .706 winning percentage and a 2.24 ERA.
In 1959 he led the Pacific Coast League with 18 wins and
a 1.87 ERA. In 1963 with the Orioles he went 5-5 with*

*12 saves and a 2.98 ERA while batting .464 (13-28). In his final 462 major league innings, he unintentionally walked only 23 batters. For his entire career, he averaged only 1.69 walks per nine innings.*

## Hank Aaron

When I first pitched at Pittsburgh, I'd throw Aaron fastballs up and in and up and away. I had pretty good success. He'd hit a fly ball, I'd get him out. Then I faced him about five or six years later in spring training, and I said, "Oh, I know how to pitch him, you just bust him, you know, up and in or up and away, a rising fastball and he hits it straight up in the air."

So the first time, I thought I'd throw him one right on the high-inside corner. Bang! Right over the left-field wall.

No, maybe I'd better pitch him up and away. So the second time up I threw him one right on the outside corner, right on top of the strike zone, and bang! He hit that over the left-center-field fence.

I said, "Oh, my!"

*Dick Hall*

# Brooks Robinson and the New World

I got traded to Baltimore in '61 from Kansas City, and the first game I was pitching, a bunt situation came up. Brooks came over and said, "You break off toward first base, 'cause I've got everything on this side."

I thought, "Oh, my, it's a new world."

Brooks used to work on his footwork. I mean, it looked spectacular, but he kind of made it look easy. Just like a long jumper, you've got to hit the board just right. Well, when you're picking up a ground ball on the run, your feet have to be exactly right, and you have to adjust your steps as you go. Most players just run and pick it up. Whatever foot they're on, then they throw. But Brooks, he used to practice it, and I realized what a difference it made.

He was the most agile I've ever seen. He could be running in and pick the ball up and throw all in one motion back to second. That kind of thing. And he had real good hands. He worked on the way he fielded the ball; he set his glove and he set his body at a certain angle so if it took a bad hop it would bounce in the dirt, and he'd pick it up and throw the guy out. After a while, you'd realize he had his glove positioned so that if it didn't hit the pocket, it didn't bounce away, and he had his body angled just right, so that if it hit his chest or something, it would bounce straight down rather than ricocheting up or something. He really made a science of it. And he had real good reflexes.

Frank Malzone probably had a stronger arm, and he had real good hands. He was a good fielder, but Brooks had the overall ability to throw on the run and throw back to second, and he had the reflexes and the footwork. Also, he had this theory: He'd play near the line, and as the pitch was made, he'd kind of lean toward the infield, which would give him a head start on a ball hit in the hole between short and third. And if it was hit down the line hard, he'd have to dive back; but he'd have time to dive, come up, and throw. And if it was hit a little bit slower, he had time to recover. So he would cheat a little bit toward the right and then kind of lean so he could cover more area to his left.

## *Playing Favorites*

Hank Bauer didn't know all the theories like Gene Mauch. The guys would complain, "Oh, he plays favorites all the time."

Somebody would point out, "Yeah, he plays favorites. He plays Brooks at third, and he plays Frank Robinson in right field. He plays Boog Powell at first. No wonder he plays favorites."

# Gail Harris

Six years (1955–1960)
Born: October 15, 1931   BL   TL   6'0"   195 lbs.
Position: First Base
New York Giants, Detroit Tigers

| G | BA | AB | H | 2B | 3B | HR | R | RBI | BB | SO | SB | FA |
|---|----|----|----|----|----|----|----|----|----|----|----|----|
| 437 | .240 | 1331 | 320 | 38 | 15 | 51 | 159 | 190 | 106 | 194 | 2 | .986 |

*A fine minor league hitter, Harris hit .314 for Lenior in 1950, .339 for Lenior and Knoxville in 1951, 23 home runs and 93 RBI for Sioux City in 1952, 25 home runs and 86 RBI for Nashville in 1953, .309 for Minneapolis in 1954 with 34 home runs and 113 RBI, and 24 home runs for Minneapolis in 1956. In his rookie year in the big leagues, 1955, he hit 12 home runs in only 263 at-bats with the Giants. Harris was traded with Ozzie Virgil to Detroit in 1958 for Jim Finigan. He hit 20 home runs, eight triples, drove in 83 runs, and batted .273 in 1958 with Detroit, his only season as a full-time player. In 1960 he was traded to the Dodgers for Sandy Amoros.*

## A Rookie's Lesson

The Cardinals had just finished batting practice, so they had time to take a couple more swings. They said, "All right, two swings everybody." Musial stayed in the cage for a couple extra swings, so this rookie they had said, "Hey, Stan, you've already had your two swings."

Slaughter picked this rookie up and put him up against the back of the cage and said, "Just shut your mouth. That could be the World Series right there hitting."

## Sense of History

I guess the biggest thrill that I ever had playing in any park was walking into Yankee Stadium. It seemed as if history just engulfed you. I'm standing there at first base, and I'm thinking, Gosh, Gehrig stood here. And this is the house that Ruth built. And then I looked out in center field and I saw the statues out there. The history of it!

# A Character, Dusty Rhodes

Dusty Rhodes of the Giants was a character, the most memorable I played with. He had ice water in his veins, did not believe there was a pitcher living who he could not hit.

"When I found out I'd passed from the second to the third grade," Dusty said, "I was so nervous, I couldn't shave."

There was a time when Dusty and I were playing in the Tri-State League, Dusty with Rock Hill, me with Knoxville. Once at Rock Hill a fan rode Dusty unmercifully. Dusty found out this fellow owned a boat dock. He took a hatchet, chopped the bottom out of the fellow's boat and got arrested. The owner of the club bailed him out. [Rhodes batted .303 and .344 his two seasons with Rock Hill and followed up with a .347 mark the next year with Nashville, so the hatchet job didn't seem to hurt his hitting.]

One day, Chuck Churn was pitching for Cincinnati, and he was throwing a spitter, so we kept hollering at the umpire to check the ball, and he wouldn't do it. So Dusty Rhodes ran out of the dugout to the mound with a bucket of water and said, "Here it is, dip it."

Of course, he was something of a clubhouse character, but I guess the thing that I remember most about Dusty was that he had ice water in his veins. He didn't think there was a pitcher that ever lived he couldn't hit. And in '54, plus the World Series, he proved it. [Rhodes batted .341 in the regular season. A World Series hero, he was 3-for-3 as a pinch hitter.]

## *Musial's Welcome*

On my first road trip, we went out to St. Louis. I'm standing by the cage during batting practice and Musial comes up and puts his arm around my shoulder. He said, "Hi, son, I'm Stan Musial. I just want to welcome you to the National League. I hope you have a good career." He was that type person. Well respected. Well thought of. He was just a good man.

## *The Lonesomest Place*

I remember my first time I batted in the big leagues was against a guy named Bob Rush, and he was throwing about a hundred miles an hour for the Cubs. Durocher sent me up to pinch hit, I'll never forget that. It was night in the Polo Grounds, and I thought, "Man, this has got to be the lonesomest place in the world." I popped out, but at least I did hit it. I hit my first home run off Lew Burdette of the Braves. I hit my last one off

Bob Turley of the Yankees. Somewhere in between, there's 49 others.

## *Have a Nice Winter*

I'll never forget a sportswriter telling me: "You know, Ted Williams hadn't spoken to me in about five years and it's the last game of the season. So I'm down in the dugout before the game, and Ted's the only player in the dugout—the rest of them are in the clubhouse— and Ted looked at me and said, 'Well, another season's about to end.' I couldn't believe he'd spoken to me, you know. And I said, 'Yeah, I guess it is.' Ted said, 'I hope you have a good winter. I hope you freeze your ass off.'"

That's just the kind of man he was, you know. But Lord, I used to go out to the ballpark there at Fenway Park early, just to watch him hit. He'd hit for an hour. And the thing he'd do—we'd always pull that shift on him, we'd have the whole infield on the right side. He didn't care. He'd try to hit right through that shift. And he would.

# Billy Hitchcock

Nine years (1942, 1946–1953)
Born: July 31, 1916   BR   TR   6'1 1/2"   185 lbs.
Positions: 3B, 240; 2B, 201; SS, 142; 1B, 48
Detroit Tigers, Washington Senators, St. Louis Browns,
Boston Red Sox, Philadelphia Athletics

| G | BA | AB | H | 2B | 3B | HR | R | RBI | BB | SO | SB | FA |
|---|-----|------|-----|----|----|----|-----|-----|-----|-----|----|------|
| 703 | .243 | 2249 | 547 | 67 | 22 | 5 | 231 | 257 | 264 | 230 | 13 | .960 |

*H*itchcock's big-league career was interruped for three years of military service. A versatile performer who played all infield positions, he appeared in more than 100 games in three seasons: 1946, 1950 (when he hit .273 in 115 games with the Athletics), and 1952. He hit .306 in 77 games for the Athletics in 1951. In 1947 he was traded with Ellis Kinder to Boston for Sam Dente, Clem Dreisewerd, Bill Sommers, and cash. After his playing *career ended, he scouted and coached for several years, managed two full seasons with the Orioles and two full seasons with the Atlanta Braves. He was president of the Southern Association from 1971 to 1980.*

## Million-Dollar Infield

I played with Kansas City in the minors. In 1940 we had Johnny Sturm at first, Gerry Priddy at second, Phil Rizzuto at short, me at third. I called it a million-dollar infield—they were worth nine hundred ninety-nine thousand and I was worth a thousand.

## Mr. Mack's Strategy

I played for Connie Mack my first year with the Athletics, in 1950. That was his last year, and he'd come down on the bench with his scorecard and his civilian suit, and he'd run the ball game for three or four innings. Then he'd leave. But he always figured that the opposing team was watching him, you know, giving the signals, so what he'd do, he'd have one of the players—and this was my first year there, I wasn't playing much—so I'd sit about two players away from him and then he'd tell me (and later on, somebody else) what to do. Dykes was the third-base coach, and he'd say, "Have him bunt." Well, I'd give Dykes the bunt signal. And he'd say, "Have him take." And I'd give Dykes the take sign. He always thought the other club was watching him with his scorecard, so that was his way of beating them.

Well, he got on a base on balls kick. His 1949 club, I guess, got a lot of bases on balls and had a good season, so he sort of got on a base on balls kick. [In 1949 the Athletics finished fifth, eight games over .500, and were second in the majors in bases on balls.] When the count went 2-0 or 3-1, he'd make some hitters take. And fellas like Fain and Zernial, they wanted to hit that cripple pitch. So we'd really try to trick Mr. Mack, and if the count went 2-0, we'd say, "You want him to hit, Mr. Mack?" and he'd say, "Let him hit, let him hit." Then when he realized what the count was, he'd say, "Make him take."

# The Proper Place for That Play

Ferris Fain was a very aggressive first baseman. He was a great fielder, and in a bunt situation he'd tell the pitcher, "You take the third-base line and I'll take everything on first base. Well, we were playing in Detroit and they got men on first and second, nobody out, and the batter bunted and Fain came almost all the way to the third-base line and fielded the ball and threw it to third—and he had a great arm, but on this particular play, he just rushed, and he threw it about four rows up into the stands.

When they came in after the inning, Mr. Mack says, "Oh, Ferris, Ferris, I don't think I would make that play like that. I don't think I'd make the play like that." Well, Ferris could really get hot, and he said, "Well, Mr. Mack, what do you want me to do with it, stick it up my ass?" And Mr. Mack said, "Ferris, that would be a very good place to put that play, yes." He was a grand old man, I'll tell you.

We went into Comisky Park, and I'm not a home run hitter or anything [In nine big league seasons, Hitchcock hit just five home runs.], but I was hitting the ball pretty good, and he hit me fourth in the lineup on that day, and the next day the Board of Directors decided it was time for Mr. Mack to retire.

# Art Houtteman

12 years (1945–1950, 1952–1957)
Born: August 7, 1927   BR   TR   6'2"   188 lbs.
Position: Pitcher
Deroit Tigers, Cleveland Indians, Baltimore Orioles

| G | W | L | PCT | ERA | GS | CG | SV | IP | H | BB | SO | BA | FA |
|---|---|---|-----|-----|----|----|----|----|---|----|----|----|----|
| 325 | 87 | 91 | .489 | 4.141 | 81 | 78 | 201 | 555 | 1646 | 516 | 639 | .193 | .963 |

*A*n All-Star in 1950 when he won 19 and saved four games for the Tigers and pitched a league-leading four shutouts, Houtteman lost 20 in 1952 after a year of military service. In 1953 he was traded with Owen Friend, Bill Wight, and Joe Ginsberg to Cleveland for Ray Boone, Al Aber, Steve Gromek, and Dick Weik. He went 15-7 and batted .277 with one home run for the pennant-winning Indians in 1954. He pitched 14 shutouts among his 78 career complete games.

104

## *Shaking Off a Sign*

In 1952, with Detroit, the year Virgil Trucks pitched his two no-hitters, I was pitching one myself against Cleveland. We had a 13-0 lead going into the ninth inning and I hadn't allowed any hits. With two outs I got two balls and one strike on a mediocre hitter, Suitcase Simpson. I shook the catcher off, and Simpson got a base hit. A little single. He was a left-handed hitter, and he hit a bouncing ball that the third baseman couldn't reach and the shortstop couldn't reach, and the ball stopped about 20 feet past the bag.

But the point is, this was the only pitch I shook Ginsberg off the whole game. He called for a curveball, and I wanted to throw a sinker. I just didn't want to throw the breaking ball he called for. What a time to make a decision, huh?

## *Discovering a New Pitch*

I discovered a sinking fastball by accident. I used to throw the fastball between the seams, the narrow part of the seams—and the ball would sail or it would sink and it would do various things. In other words, it was a live fastball. Well, being a kid on the Detroit team, not pitching much, I was pitching batting practice a lot. They had to give me work, and I could throw strikes.

105

Of course, the hitters all cried and moaned up there; especially if you're throwing white baseballs that are a little roughed up, the ball really reacts. In fact, Rudy York would come out and see me throwing batting practice, and he'd turn around and go back in the clubhouse. He'd say, "I'm not going to sting my hands, the heck with it." So I had to throw the ball during batting practice with a cross seam, which kept the ball riding straight and true. Of course, when I got in a ball game, I'd go back between the seams.

Well, what developed somehow, when I went back between the seams, the ball reacted in a different way. It just sank. I didn't even have to make any effort at all to make the ball sink, and sometimes that thing would sink 9, 10, 12 inches. And that's throwing it hard. What turned out to be a negative factor turned out to be a good one, because I could jam those right-handed hitters. And left-handed hitters would be topping it and hitting an awful lot of ground balls, which afforded me lots of chances for double plays. And they were balls that weren't going to be going out of the ballpark. So it turned out that I had to develop my pitching all around the sinking fastball.

# Sid Hudson

12 years (1940–1942, 1946–1954)
Born: January 3, 1915  BR  TR  6'4"  180 lbs.
Position: Pitcher
Washington Senators, Boston Red Sox

| G | W | L | PCT | ERA | GS | CG | SV | IP | H | BB | SO | BA | FA |
|---|---|---|-----|-----|----|----|----|-----|---|----|----|----|----|
| 380 | 104 | 152 | .406 | 4.28 | 279 | 123 | 132 | 181 | 2384 | 835 | 734 | .220 | .955 |

*A* two-time All-Star, Hudson won 40 games in his first three years with Washington while completing 55 of 95 starts. After his third season, he spent three years in the Army Air Corps and then, after some arm problems, was never the same pitcher. His best season after World War II was 1950, when he went 14-14 with 17 complete games in 30 starts for the Senators. A good hitter, he batted over .200 in eight of his first nine years, including .308 in 1947. Hudson pitched 11 shutouts and two one-hitters, *losing one no-hit bid in the ninth inning. In 1952 he was traded to the Red Sox for Randy Gumpert and Walt Masterson. He was a coach with the Senators, Red Sox, and Rangers. He was also a college pitching coach at Baylor University.*

## Lean Horse for a Long Race

I used to enjoy pitching complete games. [Hudson averaged 18 complete games a year in his first three big-league seasons.] Most pitchers did back then. Today they don't even pitch nine. They used to give me the ball and say, "Here,"—I was kind of slender—and they said, "Here, it's yours for a long race." Lean horse for a long race.

I wouldn't enjoy it today as much because they won't let you go nine innings anymore. They won't even let you. And in the American League you wouldn't get to hit. That was part of the game, being able to get a bat in your hand and hit.

## Jimmie Foxx

Jimmie Foxx hit a home run off of me the first game I ever pitched in Washington. But I had some success with him too. One time I was pitching against him up at Boston. We used to have to go through their dugout to get to our clubhouse. I started through their dugout and Jimmie was sitting there near the bat rack and he grabbed me and squeezed me into a corner and said, "I'm going to break that arm off. You're not going to sidearm me today."

There were a lot of great players in my day. I pitched against them many a time and really enjoyed them.

## *Pitching on Babe Ruth Day*

I pitched on Babe Ruth Day in New York, in Yankee Stadium, when he was dying of cancer. He was trying to give a little talk, and he was hard to understand. I pitched that game and beat Spud Chandler. I got a base hit in the seventh inning and they sacrificed me to second, and Buddy Lewis got a base hit and I scored the run, so I won the game 1-0. We had a full house. It was rather emotional. The most unusual thing is that nobody could understand him. It was a thrill to see him out there, but he had lost a lot of weight and he didn't look very good. It was kind of sad, but it was quite a thrill.

*Sid Hudson (second from left)*

# *Who Had the Better Night?*

[The only person to be elected to the baseball, college football, and pro football halls of fame, Cal Hubbard, at 6'3" and 250 pounds, was an imposing figure.]

Cal Hubbard was a great big guy, and a good umpire.

I'm pitching a game in St. Louis one night and I'm having my problems, can't get them out, and about the fourth inning they bring in somebody else. I'd been arguing with Cal all during the game, and as I leave the field, I walk by home plate and tell him, "Cal, you were terrible tonight. I never saw you miss as many pitches as you did tonight. That's the worst I ever saw you umpire."

He says, "Sid, my night must have been better than yours, because you're leaving and I'm staying."

# Ernie Johnson

Nine years (1950, 1952–1959)
Born: June 16, 1924   BR   TR   6'3 1/2"   190 lbs.
Position: Pitcher
Boston Braves, Milwaukee Braves, Baltimore Orioles

| G | W | L | PCT | ERA | GS | CG | SV | IP | H | BB | SO | BA | FA |
|---|---|---|-----|-----|----|----|----|-----|-----|-----|-----|------|------|
| 273 | 40 | 23 | .635 | 3.77 | 19 | 3 | 19 | 574.2 | 587 | 231 | 319 | .180 | .946 |

*Johnson's minor league record was 63-32 in seven seasons. He started in the minors in 1942 at Hartford, then spent three years in the military. He had a losing record only twice in 15 professional seasons, and only once in his nine big-league seasons. In 1951, with Milwaukee of the American Association, he led the league in winning percentage with a 15-4 record and in ERA at 2.62. In the major leagues he was primarily a relief pitcher, with 10 of*

*his 19 starts coming in 1952. Though he lost his only*
*decision in the 1957 World Series (Game 6 on a home run*
*by Hank Bauer), he allowed only one run on two hits in*
*seven innings of relief, striking out eight and walking only*
*one. Johnson has been a longtime broadcaster for the*
*Atlanta Braves.*

## Debut

I'll always remember my major league debut, in
1950 vs. the Phillies. I came in from the bullpen
thinking, "You made it—you made the ML."

So few do.

The batter was Dick Whitman. I was told to pitch
him low. I did and he hit the ball right between my legs
into center field for a base hit.

Welcome to the big leagues, kid.

## Size Doesn't Matter

Baseball is the greatest game in the world. It's a
sport where size doesn't count.

While growing up, both boys and girls play; that's
one of the reasons women are such great fans.

It's personal; fans can name and relate to every player—not just a few.

Spring is really here when baseball starts.

Winter is not too distant when the season ends.

# *Playing for Fred Haney*

I enjoyed Fred Haney a lot. He was our manager when we won in Milwaukee. You didn't have to be a superstar. If you did your job—say you got in a ball game and the game was lost, but you got somebody out for two or three innings, he didn't lose sight of that.

He'd walk by your locker and say, "Nice going, big guy."

He was the same to everybody. It wasn't like you had to be a star to be on his team. He treated everybody the same way.

# Spider Jorgensen

Five years (1947–1951)
Born: November 3, 1919   BL   TR   5'9"   155 lbs.
Position: Third Base  (OF, 11)
Brooklyn Dodgers, New York Giants

| G | BA | AB | H | 2B | 3B | HR | R | RBI | BB | SO | SB | FA |
|---|-----|-----|-----|----|----|----|----|-----|-----|----|----|------|
| 267 | .266 | 755 | 201 | 40 | 11 | 9 | 97 | 107 | 106 | 75 | 5 | .941 |

*J*orgensen was the Dodgers' starting third baseman in 1947 in an infield that had Reese at short, Stanky at second, and Jackie Robinson at first. He hit .274 that season and played all seven games in the Dodgers' World Series loss to the Yankees. In 1948 he hit .300 in an injury-plagued 31-game season. In 1949 he played 53 games for the Dodgers and four more games in the World Series. An arm injury shortened his career.

# '47 World Series

In the '47 Series it was tough playing in Yankee Stadium because of those shadows. Allie Reynolds was more or less throwing out of that sunlight into the shadows, and man, you couldn't see the ball. I couldn't, and everybody else couldn't. I was really nervous, tight. He threw that first pitch to me. It was about a foot over my head, and if I was nice and loose and relaxed, I'd have swung at it. But my shoulders felt like they were tied in knots, and I couldn't get up there and get it. On top of that, we didn't have a chance to work out in the stadium before the Series. Rickey and MacPhail got into some rhubarb and they said, "Well, we won't work out over there." That was a big disadvantage, I thought. [The Yankees won the first two games, played at Yankee Stadium. Specs Shea won the opener 5-3; Reynolds won the second game 10-3. The Dodgers won the next two at Ebbets Field. The Yankees won Game 5, 2-1; the Dodgers Game 6, 8-6; the Yankees Game 7, 5-2.]

I was one of the players who didn't realize Bill Bevens was throwing a no-hitter in Game 4 of the '47 Series. I really didn't think he had good stuff. He was changing up good, and we were hitting line drives all over the place, and they were right at somebody. As a matter of fact, I made the second out in the ninth inning. [The Dodgers' Cookie Lavagetto got a pinch double with two outs in the last of the ninth for the only Dodger hit. It drove in two runs and won the game 3-2. Bevens walked 11 batters.]

I scored the first Dodger run in that game. In the fifth inning I got on base on a walk and got over to third base and scored on an infield out or a sacrifice fly. I never thought Bevens had good stuff, except for his change-up.

In the seventh game we went into the lead early. [In the top of the second, the Dodgers scored their only two runs of the game and lost 5-2.] I know I had come up with two men on and I hit a double into right field that bounced into the stands. That put runners on second and third. I thought maybe Shotton should have put a pinch hitter in for Hal Gregg. [The Dodger pitcher—0-for-3 in the Series—had a .205 lifetime average.] He grounded out and that ended the inning.

But our pitching was a little short, anyway. Lavagetto said later on that if that ball I hit had not bounced into the stands and ricocheted along the fence and out into center field, I'd have had a triple and we'd have had an extra run, and it'd have made a difference in the ball game.

I remember when we finished the last game—I was staying at the St. George Hotel in Brooklyn—I said, "Oh, man, I'll be glad to get down there and get a beer under my belt and loosen up." I went down there, and all the crowd was down there, and I had a beer, and it hit my stomach like a sack of rocks. It just tasted like sour water, I couldn't drink it. I was unwinding, I guess.

# We Never Knew

When I first joined the Dodgers in 1947, Jackie Robinson was there. The team took a train to Philadelphia. The bus picked us up and took us to the hotel. We never got out. Our traveling secretary said, "Well, stay here now. I'll check here now. I'll let you know when you can get out."

So he went into the hotel—I forget what hotel it was—and finally, he came out and said, "No, we're going to another hotel."

So we went over to the Warwick. And I heard the guys saying, "Geez, this is great. Oh, man, we never stayed here before." And I never knew, really, what the deal was until about 40 years later when I read that the hotel we were supposed to stay at wouldn't allow blacks in there.

So we just jumped in and went to the Warwick Hotel, which was great. But a lot of things went on I never knew was going on because we weren't told anything.

# How to Go 5-for-5

One of the things about Musial that used to irritate the heck out of me—they'd pitch him right and he'd always bloop one into center field—hit it on the end of the bat. Somewhere. He'd always get two or three hits that way in addition to drilling the ball. That's the secret of a good hitter. You can pitch him well and you'll hit him on the fists and he'll get a bloop over first base. In Musial's case, he'd hit the ball on the end of the bat just enough to get it over the infield. He'd hit one or two like that and then he'd drill about three other ones and he'd come out 5-for-5.

## The Society of Baseball

Baseball was a great life. It still is, because I scout with the Cubs.

But one thing that kind of stands out: I can probably go to any city in the United States and mention something about baseball and say, "Oh, I played with this guy, I played with that guy."

"What's your name?"

"Spider Jorgensen."

"Oh, man, I remember you."

# Ralph Kiner

10 years (1946–1955)
Born: October 27, 1922   BR   TR   6'2"   195 lbs.
Positions: OF, 1382; 1B, 58
Pittsburgh Pirates, Chicago Cubs, Cleveland Indians

| G | BA | AB | H | 2B | 3B | HR | R | RBI | BB | SO | SB | FA |
|---|---|---|---|---|---|---|---|---|---|---|---|---|
| 1472 | .279 | 5205 | 1451 | 216 | 39 | 369 | 971 | 1015 | 1011 | 749 | 22 | .975 |

*Kiner was elected to Baseball's Hall of Fame in 1975. One of baseball's all-time great sluggers, he led the National League in home runs his first seven seasons. He hit 40 or more home runs five years in a row, scoring and driving in more than 100 runs each season. During his 10-year career, his season averages were 37 home runs, 101 RBI, and 101 walks. In June 1953, he was traded with Joe Garagiola, Howie Pollet, and Catfish Metkovich from the Pirates to the Cubs for six players and cash. Kiner's ratio of homer to at-bats is third all time. He was a six-time All-Star and was The Sporting News Player of the Year in 1950. A bad back forced his retirement at the age of 33. Kiner has been broadcasting Mets games since 1962.*

## Hitting Over 50 Home Runs

One of my real big thrills was when I hit 51 home runs in my second year. When I finally did get my 50th, of course, that was a tremendous accomplishment, as far as I was concerned. I had one stretch where I hit eight home runs in four games, which no one's ever done in baseball history.

But what I remember most about that season is that going into June 1, I had hit only three home runs. I had started the season with Hank Greenberg in spring training, and he had made some changes in my approach to hitting. In fact, Billy Herman, who was the manager of the team, went to the owner and wanted to send me back to the minors because I had not done anything for the first part of that season.

Then on June 1, I got started after a disastrous day, the last day of May, when I struck out four times against Hank Borowy. It was written in the papers that Herman wanted to send me back to the minor leagues, so I was really at the low point of my whole career.

Then, all of a sudden, everything fell in place, and I ended up hitting 48 home runs from that day to the end of the season, including 50 and 51. So that, to me, was probably the biggest part of my baseball life, that tremendous turnaround that I had and the vindication of Hank Greenberg's judgment in how to go about hitting.

Johnny Mize and I ended up in a tie, with 51, for the championship. He didn't hit one the last day and neither did I. In the course of his trying to be the leader, he hit as a leadoff batter—probably the only time in his life he ever led off—to get more times at bat; and they asked me if I wanted to be a leadoff batter, and I said, "No, I'll hit in the same spot."

I don't know really why I didn't, unless I thought it would jinx me.

The year I hit 54 home runs [1949] I was never really in a position to break Ruth's record. I was gaining on it, but the one thing I was really trying to do was to get 56 and 57 to break the National League record. But it was unrealistic for me to break Ruth's record of 60 because I hit 16 in the last month.

# *The Suspension*

The only time I was ever ejected from a ball game was in Pittsburgh. Jocko Conlan called me out on

*Ralph Kiner (left) and Hank Sauer*

a close play at first base. After running down the line, I came back to argue, along with our first-base coach. The two of us were standing almost side by side and Conlan tried to walk between us and I accidentally stepped on his foot. He wrote in the report that I had shoved and pushed him and stomped on his foot. Ford Frick, the National League president, suspended me for three days. I've got pictures of my hands being in my back pockets, and I never stomped on him at all.

The suspension was wired in to Pittsburgh on Sunday morning. We were playing Cincinnati in a doubleheader, a sellout crowd. Our general manager, Branch Rickey, wasn't at the ballpark because he never went to the ballpark on Sundays, but his son, the Twig, was there. He got the wire. He called his dad and said, "We've got a wire that Kiner is suspended for three days, the suspension starting today, and we've got all this crowd. The fans will all want their money back or there'll be a riot."

Rickey said, "Well, see if you can call up Frick and get the suspension to start on Monday." They tried to find Frick, and I don't know if they did, but the suspension was changed to start on Monday, which was an off day, so I only missed two games.

In that doubleheader against Cincinnati, I hit three home runs.

# Nellie King

Four years (1954–1957)
Born: March 15, 1928   BR   TR   6'6"   185 lbs.
Position: Pitcher
Pittsburgh Pirates

| G | W | L | PCT | ERA | GS | CG | SV | IP | H | BB | SO | BA | FA |
|---|---|---|-----|-----|----|----|----|-----|-----|----|----|------|-------|
| 95 | 7 | 5 | .583 | 3.58 | 4 | 0 | 6 | 173.1 | 193 | 50 | 72 | .000 | 1.000 |

*K*ing pitched all but four of his 95 games for the Pirates in relief, before his career was cut short by arm trouble. He had outstanding control. In almost 1,500 major and minor league innings pitched, he averaged fewer than two and a half walks per nine innings. In his final two seasons with the Pirates, he appeared in 74 games in relief with a 6-2 record and six saves. He batted 23 times for the Pirates without a hit and fielded 39

125

chances without an error. King won 20 games in 1948 for New Iberia in the Evangeline League while pitching a league-leading 284 innings. In 1953, with Denver, after two years of military service, he led the Western League in games pitched (50) and winning percentage (.833); he won 15 and lost three. In 1954, with New Orleans of the Southern Association, he went 16-5 and led the league with a 2.25 ERA. He broadcast the Pittsburgh Pirates' games for nine seasons.

## Impersonating Branch Rickey

Branch Rickey was the greatest personality I've ever known. I used to do impersonations of him. I could impersonate him well.

Branch Jr. was a great guy. Branch Sr. was in the training room in Fort Myers getting his ankles wrapped. He had a big sheet over him, lying on his back, and he had a big belly—Branch Jr. said, "Go in and do an impersonation of him."

I said, "Oh, man, I don't want to do that. I don't want to embarrass myself."

He said, "Go ahead, he'd enjoy that."

I went in there. I started in, "There's nobody I'd sooner see up with the bases loaded and the score tied in the bottom of the ninth inning but Dick Cole, but not for my team." He started to laugh a little bit.

"Bob Friend, they used to say he's got more native stuff than anybody on the staff, but, of course, he got most of it when he trained in Cuba."

He laughed, his belly started shaking. He said, "Oh, Judas Priest"—was his favorite expression—he said, "That's good, where did you learn to do that?"

I said, "Well, I've been in the organization for about nine years now. Of course, I haven't taken any money out of it."

And he said, "No, and you won't."

I don't think he was any tighter than anybody else. He was realistic in what he paid. He wasn't giving money away, certainly. But he was a great personality in the game. He could have been a great minister, or he could have been a senator. He would have been a heck of a senator. Because he had a great social conscience, you know.

He's the one who started his teams wearing the batting helmets. We wore the first ones in 1954. Those suckers were so heavy. I still have one. They tore down Forbes Field and one of the guys in the ground crew found mine there. I have it up there to give to my daughter. But boy, those suckers were heavy, hard plastic. Your neck would get sore. He made all the pitchers wear them all the time, in the field and at bat. Everybody had to wear them.

# The Psychology of Warming Up

The first game I ever pitched in the big leagues was in Ebbets Field.

Warming up—in baseball it's psychological a lot of times; if you pick up a ball and it feels light, you feel stronger. The other thing, if you're feeling strong, you stand on the mound and the catcher looks like he's about 45 feet away, not 60. And I started to throw, and these two things were there—the ball was light and the catcher looked like he was on me, and I started throwing strikes, and my fastball started to move. The catcher was dropping everything I'm throwing, so I'm really on a high; and we scored three runs, so the inning lasted longer than normal. I had gone down to the dugout after warming up, and I sat with my roommate and he said, "How do you feel?" I said, "I feel pretty good. My fastball's moving, the ball feels light, I feel strong, I'm throwing curveballs and throwing strikes, and the catcher's dropping everything I'm throwing." He said, "Who's catching?" I said, "Vic Janowicz." He said, "Oh, he can't catch anybody." I didn't want to hear that because I thought, "Maybe I wasn't throwing that hard."

I took my jacket off and I walked off to the mound, my first time in the big leagues, and I picked up the ball, turned around to look at home plate, and I thought, "I must be standing on second base." It seemed so far away. The double-deck stands, the whole thing, just completely, psychologically disoriented me. It was like you have binoculars and you're looking at the wrong end. And I said to myself, "I don't think I can throw the ball from here to there without bouncing it." I wasn't feeling too comfortable.

Duke Snider was the hitter. I threw him a sinker outside. He fouled it. A ball. I threw him a curveball inside and he fouled that. I had him 1-and-2, and I threw him a fastball low and away, and for some reason, he tried to bunt it and he fouled it, and I said, "Holy cow, I struck him out!" He struck himself out by trying to bunt. It was the last time he ever did that. I got out of the inning, I gave up one hit, and they didn't score a run. I clipped every box score out of every paper in New York that day. 'Cause I knew if I didn't pitch again, that's proof that I did pitch in the big leagues; it was in there. But it's amazing how disorienting it can be.

# Frank Dascoli

[Dascoli, a respected National League umpire for 15 years, had the distinction of kicking out basketball star Bill Sharman, who had been called up by the Dodgers. Sharman left with the other Dodgers when Dascoli cleared the bench. Thus Sharman is the only player ever to be ejected from a big-league game without appearing in one. King remembers Dascoli for another reason.]

Bobby Bragan [the Pirates' manager] used to do things like throw stuff out on the field and lie on home plate, and they had to drag him off. He always made some headlines, had the title of umpire-baiter, and the umpires wanted to make sure this guy didn't pull any crap in the major leagues. Dascoli was a pretty good ball-and-strike umpire, but he was kind of naive. We're playing in Ebbets Field in a Saturday afternoon game. Our pitcher was getting bumped around a little bit, and Bragan was going to make a change. He came out to the mound and all the infielders were around there.

He says, "Just stay here for a while, Dascoli will be out pretty soon."

Dascoli comes out and says, "You going to make a decision?"

Bragan says, "I don't know." He asks the third baseman, George Freese, "What do you think, George? Should we yank him?"

George says, "Oh, I don't know, he looks like he's throwing pretty good to me. His fastball looks pretty fast from this angle."

He asks Dick Groat, and Dick says, "Oh, no, his fastball's not moving. It's quick, but it's not moving."

Gene Freese was playing second. "What do you think, Gene?"

"No, his fastball's not moving at all. You better take him out."

He asks Dale Long, "What do you think, Dale?"

"No, I go along with George. It looks like he's throwing pretty good."

And he turns around and says to Frank Dascoli, "What do you think we should do, Frank?"

Dascoli says, "Oh, I can't make that decision for you. You're in the big leagues now, you've got to make that decision yourself. I can't tell you what to do."

Dascoli didn't know he was getting his chain pulled.

# Musial's Magic

I remember throwing Musial a little sinker, low and outside. He hit a fly ball to deep right-center field, and they ran it down. He came up the next time and I threw him the same pitch and he hit a double down the left-field line. He knew what I was doing, you know. So I suddenly realized, well, I don't think he's going to pull that pitch, so I better come in on him. Instead of going away I came in with a fastball and he hit a double off the right-field screen. I said, "Hey, I don't have anything else. I already pitched him outside, he got a double on it. Came in on him, he hits a double off the screen in right field."

Musial was the best player I played against. I'd compare him to Babe Ruth because he played over such a long span of time and in conditions that were constantly changing. He played before World War II when it was mostly daytime ball and only white players played. He played after the war when blacks and Latinos came into the game. He played when night baseball took over. He played when expansion to the west coast came in and plane flights (prop planes and eight-hour trips to the coast) became necessary. He also played when the National League enlarged from eight to 10 teams. Nobody produced the records he did during a period where baseball changed so much.

# Johnny Klippstein

18 years (1950–1967)
Born: October 17, 1927   BR   TR   6'1"   173 lbs.
Position: Pitcher
Chicago Cubs, Cincinnati Reds, Los Angeles Dodgers,
Cleveland Indians, Washington Senators, Philadelphia Phillies,
Minnesota Twins, Detroit Tigers

| G | W | L | PCT | ERA | GS | CG | SV | IP | H | BB | SO | BA | FA |
|---|---|---|-----|-----|----|----|----|----|----|----|----|----|----|
| 711 | 101 | 118 | .461 | 4.24 | 162 | 37 | 66 | 1967.2 | 1915 | 978 | 1158 | .125 | .966 |

*K*lippstein pitched professionally from 1944 to 1967. *In 1965 he joined with Al Worthington in the Minnesota Twins' bullpen to help the Twins win the AL pennant. He pitched 56 games in relief that year, going 9-3 with five saves and a 2.24 ERA. With Cleveland in 1960, he appeared in 49 games with a 2.91 ERA, going 5-5 with a league-leading 14 saves. In 1963 he had a 1.93 ERA for the Phillies in 49 games. In 1958 he was* traded with Steve Bilko from the Reds to the Dodgers for Don Newcombe. From 1958 to 1964 he pitched for six different teams. Of his 101 big league wins, 59 came in relief. During his first eight seasons, he pitched both as a starter and a reliever, starting 149 games, but in his last 10 seasons, only 13 of his last 396 appearances were as a starter.

## Playing for Alston and Tebbetts

Walter Alston was a quiet man who got things done by saying very little, but everybody had great respect for him, and I think he had great knowledge when it came to handling a pitching staff. And I think that was most of his success, being able to handle people and keep them in line and keep everybody happy, and also being able to handle a pitching staff.

I think that Birdie Tebbetts, on the other hand, was a great psychologist. He had a way with people. I remember in '56, when we almost won the pennant, we finished two games out. He had a meeting with the pitchers before the season started, and he said, "Well, fellows, I don't care what the newspapers write; we've got a better pitching staff than what they say, and we can win this thing because you guys would run through the wall for me."

What we didn't know was about three weeks later he called all the hitters in—infielders, outfielders, and catchers—and said, "Fellows, you know what kind of a

*Johnny Klippstein*

pitching staff we have. We're going to have to score a lot of runs."

We ended up having a pretty good ball club that year. We came up a little short, but we came within two games of winning the thing. But he was a pretty good guy to play for. I thought he was a ballplayer's manager.

# For the Good of the Team

When I was with the Reds in 1956, I was pitching a no-hitter against the Braves. After seven innings, we were behind 1-0 due to bases on balls and a sacrifice fly. In the top of the eighth, Birdie Tebbetts took me out for a pinch hitter. Hershell Freeman relieved me and then Joe Black relieved Hershell. We still had a no-hitter after nine innings. We tied the game 1-1 in the ninth and lost it 2-1 in the 10th.

Almost everyone I talked to thought Birdie should have let me go for the no-hitter, but I didn't feel bad at all when he took me out because we were fighting to win the pennant. I felt that whenever the individual player becomes bigger than the game itself, you have a problem.

Baseball's a team game.

# Bob Kuzava

10 years (1946–1947, 1949–1955, 1957)
Born: May 28, 1923   BB   TL   6'2"   202 lbs.
Position: Pitcher
Cleveland Indians, Chicago White Sox, Washington Senators,
New York Yankees, Baltimore Orioles, Philadelphia Phillies,
Pittsburgh Pirates, St. Louis Cardinals

| G | W | L | PCT | ERA | GS | CG | SV | IP | H | BB | SO | BA | FA |
|---|---|---|-----|-----|----|----|----|----|----|----|----|----|----|
| 213 | 49 | 44 | .527 | 4.05 | 99 | 34 | 13 | 862 | 849 | 415 | 446 | .086 | .942 |

*In 1942 Kuzava led the Middle Atlantic League with 21 wins for Charleston; then he spent three years in the military, where he rose to the rank of sergeant. He reached the big leagues with Cleveland in 1946 and was traded to the White Sox in 1948. He won 10 games for the White Sox in 1949 and 11 for the Senators and Yankees in 1951. He was traded with Cass Michaels and John Ostrowski from the White Sox to the Senators in 1950 for*

*Al Kozar, Ray Scarborough, and Eddie Robinson. In 1951 he was traded from the Senators to the Yankees for Fred Sanford, Tom Ferrick, and Bob Porterfield. Of his 49 wins with the Yankees, 23 came between 1951 and 1954. He pitched in the 1951, '52, and '53 World Series, saving the final games of the '51 and '52 Series. He was used mostly as a reliever in his last four seasons, with 69 of his last 87 appearances coming in relief. In one of his six starts in 1953, he lost a no-hit bid in the ninth inning. Kuzava pitched seven shutouts in his 99 big-league starts.*

# '51 World Series

I was lucky enough to save the final game in two World Series. In 1951, I got the final out with the tying run on second. Sal Yvars hit a line drive off me to Hank Bauer, our right fielder. I had played against Sal for about two years in the International League in 1947 and '48, and he always hit the ball pretty good. He was a right-handed hitter, but he used to hit it the other way. He hit a hard, sinking line drive off me, and Bauer made a nice running catch in short right field in Yankee Stadium. He caught the ball maybe waist high. If it had been hit three feet either way, it'd have been a double. But it was right at Hank and that was the end of the Series. [The Yankees won the game 4-3, and won the Series four games to two.]

In the seventh game of the '52 Series, we were beating the Dodgers in Ebbets Field 4-2, but they loaded the bases with one out in the seventh inning. Stengel brought me in to pitch to Snider, because I had pitched against him in the minor leagues, and he was a left-hander. I popped Snider up to Rizzuto and said to myself, "Well, I did my job; now I can go sit on the bench and root for the guys." Johnny Sain, a right-hander, was warming up in the bullpen, and I figured Casey would bring him in to pitch to Jackie Robinson, because the Dodgers sure weren't going to pinch-hit for Jackie. Well, Casey left me in there. I figured he had faith in me getting Jackie out. I got him to pop up in the infield; that was the dramatic catch that Billy Martin made. [Racing in at full speed, Martin made a lunging catch near the mound.] Joe Collins, our first baseman, lost the ball in the sun, so I got out of the way and hollered for Billy, but that was to no avail because nobody could hear me; everybody was screaming. Billy was playing deep because there were two outs and he wanted to be able to knock the ball down if it was hit on the ground. With two outs, everybody was running, and they all would have scored if Billy hadn't made the catch. Collins was one of the best first basemen in the league, and ordinarily, he would have caught the ball easily, but hey, you can't catch it if you can't see it. Casey kept me in to finish the game, and I retired all eight batters I faced. We won the game 4-2.

# *Almost on the Ed Sullivan Show*

We were playing the White Sox in Yankee Stadium August 8, 1953, and I was pitching against Virgil Trucks. I had a no-hitter with one out in the ninth inning. Bob Boyd, a little left-handed hitter with the White Sox, hit a line drive over Billy Martin's head, a clean hit, for a double, and I got the next two guys out. I threw the pitch where I wanted it to Boyd, down and in, a strike on the inside part of the plate. And he hit the ball good. I'm glad he did. I'm glad he didn't bloop it or something. You take your hat off to him. To get a no-hitter you've got to earn it. He got a base hit and he earned it.

I knew I had a no-hitter going. Anybody who's pitching a no-hitter—if they tell you they don't know it, they're kidding you. The dugout was pretty normal, but nobody talks to you very much when you're going with a no-hitter—they kind of leave you alone. They believe it's bad luck to mention it. Everybody in the park knows you've got a no-hitter going, plus you. They're all pulling for you, naturally.

It was Ladies' Day, I can remember that, and there were about 70,000 people there. I won the ball game three to nothing, I think. I got a one-hitter, but it cost me some money. Because that was a Saturday, and the next night I could probably have been on "The Ed Sullivan Show" if I'd pitched a no-hitter. If you pitched a no-hitter in those days, you usually picked up a few bucks by going on Ed Sullivan's show.

# Max Lanier

14 years (1938–1946, 1949–1953)
Born: August 18, 1915   BR   TL   5'11"   180 lbs.
Position: Pitcher
St. Louis Cardinals, New York Giants, St. Louis Browns

| G | W | L | PCT | ERA | GS | CG | SV | IP | H | BB | SO | BA | FA |
|---|---|---|---|---|---|---|---|---|---|---|---|---|---|
| 327 | 108 | 82 | .568 | 3.01 | 204 | 91 | 17 | 1618.1 | 1490 | 611 | 821 | .185 | .959 |

*L*anier was a two-time All-Star (1943–1944). He
pitched 21 career shutouts. He won a total of 45
games for the three consecutive pennant-winning Cardinal
teams of 1942–1944. He was 6-0 in 1946 with a 1.90
ERA, when he jumped to the Mexican League, causing his
suspension from organized baseball.  Reinstated in 1949,
he won 11 games for the Cardinals in both 1950 and
1951. In seven World Series games, he was 2-1 with a
1.71 ERA in 31 2/3 innings. Lanier won Game 4 of the

*1942 Series and the sixth (and decisive) game of the 1944
Series. His son Hal was a major league player, coach, and
manager.*

# Pepper Martin

Pepper Martin was always playing practical jokes. He
liked to load up cigarettes and cigars. Buzzy Wares
was our first-base coach, and Pepper had put a loaded
bunch of matches in his pocket, and when he pulled
them out and struck the match, it all fired up in front
of his face and he said, "I'll use my own matches." He
was smoking a cigar, and as he lit the cigar, that blew
up, too, and everybody laughed. Even the manager
laughed then, and he was pretty serious most of the
time. Pepper did things like that all the time.

Once, we were in Chicago, and Frankie Frisch
was the manager. They had a big staircase that led to
the second floor, so you didn't have to take the elevator.
Pepper had a big balloon full of water, and he saw
Frankie Frisch outside walking, and he dropped it out
the window. He ran down the stairs and sat in the
lobby and was reading a newspaper by the time Frisch
got in the hotel lobby.

Frisch said, "I'd have swore that was you that put
that water on me if I didn't see you sitting here."

*Max Lanier*

# A Scorer's Philosophy

In the first inning of a game in St. Louis against the Braves, a guy hit a ball to Whitey Kurowski and it bounced up and it hit him in the chest and they gave him a hit on it. That was the only hit they got off me.

The scorekeeper came to me the next day and said, "Max, if it had been in the fifth inning, I'd have given you a no-hitter."

I said, "Well, I don't know what the difference is between the first inning and the fifth inning."

# You and Me Again

Babe Pinelli was one of my favorites. It seemed like he umpired half of my ball games. I'd be warming up—we warmed up in front of our dugout before then. He'd come out with a mask in his hand and say, "Looks like it's you and me again, Max."

I'd say, "That's good enough for me."

# Bob Lennon

Three years (1954, 1956–1957)
Born: September 15, 1928   BL   TL   6'0"   200 lbs.
Position: Outfield
New York Giants, Chicago Cubs

| G | BA | AB | H | 2B | 3B | HR | R | RBI | BB | SO | SB | FA |
|---|---|---|---|---|---|---|---|---|---|---|---|---|
| 38 | .165 | 79 | 13 | 2 | 0 | 1 | 5 | 4 | 5 | 26 | 0 | .900 |

*L*ennon had one of the greatest minor league seasons in
history with Nashville of the Southern Association in
1954 (64 home runs, 161 RBI, 139 runs scored, 210 hits,
and a .345 batting average). He hit 31 home runs with
104 RBI for Minneapolis of the American Association in
1955. (Six more home runs in the playoffs helped Minneapolis to the Little World Series crown.)  In 1960 he
helped lead Montreal to the International League pennant, with 28 home runs and 89 RBI. He stole 19 bases
in 1946, his first full season in the minors. He played nine

*years in the minors before getting a shot at the majors. His major league career was cut short by arm trouble (a pinched nerve). Lennon was traded with Dick Littlefield from the Giants to the Cubs in 1957 for Ray Jablonski and Ray Katt.*

## Working on the Farm Team

I was only 16 when the Dodgers signed me. My father was a New York City policeman. My uncle was, too. They were sitting in the kitchen with me, telling me, "You're going down on the farm team. You're going to have to go out and pick tomatoes and cabbage or whatever they have planted every day, and work all day long in the fields and play baseball every night. It's not going to be easy."

I believed them. I said, "I don't care."

I think I got 90 dollars a month, my first contract.

But I believed them when they were kidding me, telling me all that.

## A Father's Expectations

My father saw me hit three home runs in one

minor league game. I also struck out three times. George Leonard, a sportswriter, said to my father, "Well, I guess you're pretty proud of your son."

My father said, "Heck, he struck out three times."

# *Brushbacks: A Part of the Game*

I got thrown at a lot. Like they say, you hit off your butt a lot. I never got hit in the head, thank God, but I've been hit all over the right side from the shoulder on down to the ankles. But it was part of the game then.

Big Bill Taylor was at Nashville one year, and I was hitting in back of him, and he hit a home run off a guy. I came up, and the pitcher knocked me down, and then I got up, and he knocked me down again, and then the next one, I just threw my bat on the ground— skidded it out there at him, and we rolled around out there for a while.

One time in Toronto I hit a home run, and the pitcher knocked me down my next time up. I hit another home run, and then the next time up, he knocked me down again. Then I hit one off the center- field fence for a double. He turned around to me and said, "Aw, I give up."

# *Voodoo Medicine*

I went to winter ball and I jammed my ankle in the playoffs sliding into third base. The owner of the club was the dictator there, and his brother-in-law owned our club, so he was giving money out, like five dollars for a single, 10 dollars for a double, 30 for a triple, I think 40 for a homer. I think 10 dollars for a run batted in. Ten for a run scored. I hit one off the center-field wall and was going for an extra 10 dollars. The guy had me at third base by 20 feet, and so I was going to slide one way and then I tried to fake him out and my ankle went the other way.

I ripped all the ligaments, and the next day, they sent me to a voodoo doctor out in the boondocks there and I couldn't even put my weight on it at all. And he gave me a lot of voodoo stuff. I started to laugh, but I had an interpreter with me.

He said, "You have to believe in this." The guy was about 80 years old.

I said, "Okay."

So after he did that, he wanted me to stamp my foot down, and I said, "I can't." So anyway, then I went home and went to spring training with the Giants and I couldn't run on it. And I hurt my throwing arm. I woke up with my arm hurting, and it's been that way ever since. It's still very bad. I continued to play until '61. When I got traded to the Cubs, they had me playing center field. 'Course, I was trying to throw, but I just couldn't.

# Don Liddle

Four years (1953–1956)
Born: May 25, 1925   BL   TL   5'10"   165 lbs.
Position: Pitcher
Milwaukee Braves, New York Giants, St. Louis Cardinals

| G | W | L | PCT | ERA | GS | CG | SV | IP | H | BB | SO | BA | FA |
|---|---|---|-----|-----|----|----|----|-----|-----|-----|-----|-----|-----|
| 117 | 28 | 18 | .609 | 3.75 | 54 | 13 | 4 | 427.2 | 397 | 203 | 198 | .152 | .946 |

*L*iddle pitched three shutouts for the world-champion
New York Giants in 1954. He started and won the
final game of the 1954 World Series against Cleveland, 7-
4, yielding just one earned run in seven innings. He threw
the pitch to Vic Wertz on which Willie Mays made his
memorable catch in the 1954 World Series. Fifty-four of
his games were as a starter, 67 as reliever. He was traded
to New York with Johnny Antonelli in 1954 for Bobby
Thomson. He was part of the eight-player trade between

the Giants and the Cardinals in 1956 involving Red
Schoendienst and Alvin Dark.

## *Play Ball: Game 1, 1954 World Series, Polo Grounds; Attendance: 52,751*

In the opening game of the 1954 World Series,
Giants left-hander Don Liddle relieved Sal Maglie in
the eighth inning with the score tied 1-1. Vic Wertz
was batting with two men on. Don and his wife, Margaret, tell of that day.

> General MacArthur came to see me pitch.
> He wore his Homburg hat.
> He leaned eagerly forward
> As Vic Wertz came up to bat.
>
> Shipwreck Kelly, Jackie Gleason,
> Spencer Tracy, Danny Kaye—
> All as nervous as this pitcher
> When the ball came into play.
>
> Baseball to America
> Is as traditional as our flag.
> Each cosmopolite debating,
> "Did he really make the tag?"

Mrs. Gehrig was present,
The whole field within her view.
As she looked down the first-base line
Memories came flooding of her Lou.

Bob Hope was watching, silent.
Not one tiny famous quip.
Not even Bob dared argue
Or second guess The Lip.

Wertz was eager ready.
He calmly took his stance,
Hoping men on first and second
His bat would now advance.

Pitch him high and tight they said.
That took away my curve.
So when Wes Westrum gave the signal
I threw that fastball with all my verve.

Is this pitcher ready?
Every eye is on the ball.
Who would guess by Say Hey Willie
They'd see the Greatest Catch of All?

# '54 World Series

In Ken Burns' baseball documentary, Bob Costas made a statement about Willie Mays' catch that I'd like to clear up. I'd been brought in to face Vic Wertz, and, of course, he hit that long ball that Willie caught. Wertz was the only man I faced.

They showed the catch, and Bob Costas said I told the relief pitcher who came in for me, Marv Grissom, "I got my man," after the catch. Well, I didn't say that there. We were still in hot water. We still had two men on, the score tied in the eighth inning, and only one man out. Well, that wouldn't have been any time to say something like that. I said it in the clubhouse after Dusty Rhodes won the game with a home run.

We were all in the clubhouse and Leo was over by Willie Mays and me. Willie and I lockered next to each other. We were all happy, and I told Leo, I said, "Well, I got my man." It was a joke, of course, because it was only because of Willie's great catch, and everybody laughed.

Well, Leo's the one that spread that around. Well, then it got turned around, that I said it to the relief pitcher coming out to the mound.

But a lot of people did the job, and I think it takes the whole 25 players to get the job done.

# *A Barber Pole Pitch*

I never had any problem with injuries. But once in the minor leagues somebody slammed a door on my hand, pinched my fingers. It caught me on the fingernails on my left hand. I went out and tried to pitch that night and I broke them loose and then it started bleeding under my fingernail and I had blood all over the ball. I couldn't keep my fingers from bleeding.

It looked like a barber pole going up there, and I had to come out of the ball game.

# Danny Litwhiler

11 years  (1940–1944, 1946–1951)
Born: August 31, 1916   BR   TR   5'10 1/2"   198 lbs.
Position: Outfield  (3B, 20)
Philadelphia Phillies, St. Louis Cardinals, Boston Braves,
Cincinnati Reds

| G | BA | AB | H | 2B | 3B | HR | R | RBI | BB | SO | SB | FA |
|------|------|------|-----|-----|----|-----|-----|-----|-----|-----|----|------|
| 1057 | .281 | 3494 | 982 | 162 | 32 | 107 | 428 | 451 | 299 | 377 | 11 | .981 |

*A*n All-Star in 1942, Litwhiler was traded to the
Cardinals in 1943 with Earl Naylor and played in
the 1943 and '44 World Series with the Cardinals. As a
rookie with the Phillies in 1940, he hit .345 in 36 games.
In his first full season, 1941, he hit .305 with a career-
high 18 home runs. Knee injuries severely hampered his
career, and after 1944, he played in a hundred games only
twice. In 1942 he became the first outfielder in history to
play at least 150 games without committing an error. In

154

*1943 he had only one error in 116 games. He also was a longtime college baseball coach for Florida State and Michigan State universities.*

## Hitting into the Wind

I had some great days and some bad days, but I had more bad days than Musial did. I played in Shibe Park, and I knew that field real well, the wind and everything. When you're in ballparks, you study the wind quite a bit, and the sun. One time I came back to Philadelphia when I was with the Cardinals, and the wind was blowing in from left field. I said to Musial, "Well, there'll be no home runs hit in left field today."

Stan said, "Why?"

I said, "When that flag's coming in like that, there's nothing gets in there unless it's a shot, a real line shot." They had two decks in left field. When the wind blew hard over there, it created a suction like a backdraft into the stands, but to get it in there, you had to just blast the ball, and you very seldom saw home runs in that wind.

"Eh," he says, "I'll hit one in there."

I said, "You do, I'll kiss your rear end right on home plate."

I'd forgotten all about it by the fifth, sixth, seventh inning, something like that, when Musial came up. He hit a blue darter out to left field, and—zoom!—right into the lower deck. He came in, and he said,

"Hey, Litwhiler, want to do it now or wait until after the game?"

# *Chuck Klein and the Thousand Milers*

I am from Pennsylvania, and my idol, when I was a kid, was Chuck Klein of the Phillies. He was having outstanding years, and I always thought, "Boy, I'd like to be like Chuck Klein." Chuck Klein batted left-handed, and I could look in a mirror and swing a bat and think I was left-handed. I pretended to be Chuck Klein. [Klein, a Hall of Famer, played from 1928 to 1944. He had a lifetime average of .320 and hit 300 home runs. He led the National League one or more times in batting average, slugging percentage, hits, doubles, home runs, runs, runs batted in, pinch hits, and stolen bases. Klein was 35 when Litwhiler was a 23-year-old rookie in 1940.]

Well, I wound up with the Phillies. Guess who my roommate was? Chuck Klein. He was great. We were in spring training my first year and were ready to go north by bus from spring training. We'd play Washington in five, six cities on the way north.

Chuck said, "Come on, roomie. Let's go get a couple Thousand Milers."

I said, "What do you mean?"

He said, "You've got to have a couple Thousand Milers; we're going to be in that bus for over a week. It's two thousand miles to get to Philadelphia, so we get a thousand miles a shirt. So we've got to go get two Thousand Milers; we'll get a black one or a blue one or a dark brown one."

So we went in, and sure enough, I got a dark blue one and a dark brown one. He got a black one and some other color. We got our Thousand Milers. Two shirts got us all the way to Philadelphia.

# A Storybook Finish

I had a great spring training with the Phillies in 1940, and it looked like I was really going to be a player. We opened up at New York, the Polo Grounds, and I wasn't playing. I couldn't figure out why. I couldn't figure it out. Then we got back home and we played two games and I still didn't play.

Finally, we played Brooklyn and I got to pinch-hit against Hugh Casey in the ninth inning. Two men out, a man on first, and we're down by one run. Well, I figured if I can hit a home run or somehow keep the thing going, maybe everything will be fine for me. I can still see the curveball Hugh Casey hung for me. It said, "Here, hit me."

I had a good cut at it, and I popped it up—one of those major league pop-ups—and before it came down, I was sent to Baltimore.

*Danny Litwhiler*

## Wearing Out Blackwell

I didn't get into the platooning with the Cardinals, but I did with the Boston Braves. Southworth believed in left and right. I was playing every day in spring training. We started coming north. We played Cincinnati in Jacksonville, and Blackwell's pitching. Billy always put the lineup up on the bulletin board; he didn't tell you at a meeting or anything that so-and-so's playing. He just put up the lineup, and you'd go out and look at the lineup and see if you're playing. So I went out and looked at the lineup and I wasn't there.

I said, "Billy, how come I'm not playing?"

He said, "Blackwell's pitching."

I said, "Well, so what?  I've been playing every day."

But he said, "Blackwell.  He's tough on right-handers."

I said, "Well, he never gave me any trouble."

He said, "He didn't?"

I said, "No." Of course, I'd never played against him, I could say that.

"Well," he said, "I'd prefer to go with a left-hander against him."

So he started a left-hander, and about the seventh, eighth inning, we're not doing anything against Blackwell, and he wanted a pinch hitter for the pitcher, and he looked in the dugout and he yelled, "Hey, Bama."

That's Bama Rowell, who was a left-hander. "Grab your bat."

Bama said, "No, no, no, no, no. Litwhiler, get your bat." [Carvel Rowell, born in Alabama, played six big league seasons, hitting .275, including 15-for-60 as pinch hitter.]

159

I thought, "Boy, here I go." So I got my bat and I get up, and Blackwell came from third base on a ball and I kind of sidestepped back and I took a good cut at it and hit it off the end of the bat. It went right over first base, and I wound up on third base, sliding in for a triple.

Southworth said, "Boy, you really do wear him out, don't you."

# How to Hurt a Guy

When I was with the Braves, Ewell Blackwell pitched a no-hitter against us. After the game, I was with my roomie, Bob Elliott. Bob would never give anybody credit for getting him out.

He said, "Oh, he didn't have anything. I don't know how he got me out."

That went on.

He said, "Let's get something to eat."

We went out to eat. He ate half a sandwich and said, "Let's go. Let's go to bed."

So we went up to the room. He's got his pajamas on, and he's sitting on the bed and he's got his head in his hands and he's yelling, "Oh for four! Oh for four!" and I said, "Bob, so what? Oh for four. I went oh for four."

He said, "Yeah, but you're used to it."

# Blackwell's No-Hitter

In 1947 Ewell Blackwell won 16 in a row with Cincinnati. He's in that streak, he's pitching on a clear night in Cincinnati, and they had a packed house, a full house, and the Braves are playing the Reds. Well, the whole night he just had it. He'd just throw the ball—it was a cool, clear night, a silent night, almost—and when he'd throw the ball, you'd hear his fingers snap and you'd hear the ball—ptt-choo, boom!—into the glove. You could just hear the whole thing. And in doing it, he shut us out, and he threw a no-hitter. [Blackwell turned the trick on June 18, 1947. The Reds won 6-0.]

The only guy who hit that night was Bama Rowell. He hit the ball every time he was up. I mean, he blasted the ball. But they're making great catches on him. Now there's two men out in the ninth inning and a no-hitter on the line, and up comes Bama Rowell. All the fans know he's been hitting the ball, and Blackie knows he's hitting the ball, and Bama knew he's hitting the ball, so the chances are that he might get a good base hit. So he's up there and the fans are cheering, and he's bouncing around and Blackwell throws the ball, and he hit a shot right down by Ted Kluszewski. Ted makes a grab for it, but he doesn't get his glove on it. Had he got his glove on it, it would have been a base hit, I think. You couldn't have given him an error, the way it was hit. But he didn't touch it, and as it went by his glove, it just went foul by about three or four inches on the grass in the outfield behind first base. And, of course, the fans are "ohh, yea!"—they've got it going again.

Well, the count is finally 3-and-2, and he blasts another one; and this time it's gone, it's a home run all the way. It just looked like a home run. And the farther it went, the more it seemed to curve. It went foul by about one foot. And, of course, the fans were cheering now because it's still 3-and-2, and Blackie's got him, so Blackie uncorked a fastball. I mean, he really threw a ball right by him. Bama comes in and he said, "That ball done riz. It did, it done riz."

# Sharp Dresser

Al Barlick was working a game in Shibe Park behind home plate and went down to make the ball-and-strike calls and he ripped his pants right from the top of his belt down into his crotch. Every time he'd go down, part of his long underwear would show and the fans would scream and just have a fit. Finally, somebody told him.

The other umpires said, "It's okay, go ahead in and change. We'll substitute for you until you get out."

He said, "No way. I'm working. I came here, and I'm getting paid to do this job, and I'm going to do it."

He did that whole ball game with his rear end sticking out.

# Marty Marion

13 years (1940–1950, 1952–1953)
Born: December 1, 1917   BR   TR   6'2"   170 lbs.
Position: Shortstop (3B, 2)
St. Louis Cardinals, St. Louis Browns

| G | BA | AB | H | 2B | 3B | HR | R | RBI | BB | SO | SB | FA |
|------|------|------|------|-----|----|----|-----|-----|-----|-----|----|------|
| 1572 | .263 | 5506 | 1448 | 272 | 37 | 36 | 602 | 624 | 470 | 537 | 35 | .969 |

*A seven-time All-Star, Marion was the NL MVP in 1944. He played on four pennant-winning and three world-championship Cardinal teams. Considered the best defensive shortstop of his day, he averaged 140 games during his first nine seasons in spite of a bad back that plagued him throughout much of his career. A consistent hitter, he batted between .272 and .280 in six of his first nine seasons. He also managed the Cardinals, Browns, and White Sox.*

163

# A Pint of Blood

One time Leo Durocher said, "Kurowski, Marion, Schoendienst, and Musial. You couldn't get a pint of blood out of the whole infield." We were so skinny. [Marion was 6'2", 170; Schoendienst was 6', 170; Musial was 6', 175; Kurowski was 5'11", 193.]

# A Hard Guy to Manage

Satchel Paige was probably the best pitcher who was ever in the Negro leagues, but when I managed Satchel Paige, he was what, 50, 60 years old? He was the hardest guy I ever had to manage, because he had his own way of doing things, and he wouldn't change it.

And Bill Veeck wouldn't change anything with Satch; he loved Satchel, you know. Sugar Cain, one of my pitchers, said one time, "Marty, why can't I do what Satchel Paige does? You know, he don't run, he don't do this, he don't do that?"

I said, "Well, Cain,"—the only answer I could think of was—"Well, when you get his age, you can do the same thing."

*Marty Marion*

# Nobody's Indispensable

During the war years, we didn't have some of the stars. They were in the army. But it didn't seem to matter. I mean, nobody ever thought about things like that. We were just playing baseball and didn't get involved with personalities. You can play a baseball game without having a Musial or a DiMaggio or a Williams or a Marion. He's not going to make the ball game any better; it's just the fans' perception that he's better. There's nobody indispensable. You can take the best baseball player, I don't know who he is, but if he didn't play baseball next year, who really cares?

# Late Bloomer

I played four years in the minors. I played in Huntington, West Virginia, in 1936, my first year. Then I played three years in Rochester, '37, '38, and '39, then came to the Cardinals in 1940.

I wasn't very good in the minor leagues, I'll tell you that right now. I was just a so-so ballplayer. I was a better major league ballplayer than I was a minor league ballplayer. I don't have any ideas why. Experience, maybe. And I got stronger. But I was better once I got to the big leagues.

# Cardinal Pitchers

The Cardinal pitchers were all good. Mort Cooper was a great pitcher, and he won what, 20, 22 games a couple of years. [From 1942 to 1944, Cooper won 22, 21, and 22 games for the Cardinals.] He could throw hard. But every time Mort pitched, we must have scored 10 or 12 runs. Every game he pitched. [Not that he needed many runs; his ERA those three years was 1.78, 2.30, and 2.46.] And then there was Max Lanier. Poor Maxie. He was just as good a pitcher as Mort Cooper, but he would walk up and down the dugout saying, "Boys, just give me one run. Please, give me a run." We couldn't score for him for nothing. So you know how the ball bounces. [In the same three seasons Lanier won 13, 15, 17, with ERAs of 2.98, 1.90, and 2.65.] Mort Cooper was a pretty good hitter, so he kind of helped himself, although Maxie wasn't a bad hitter, either. [Cooper hit .194 lifetime; Lanier, .185.] Pitchers do help themselves in the lineup where you don't have the designated hitter.

Howard Pollet was my roommate for years. He was a wonderful man, a very religious man, and a hell of a pitcher. Harry Brecheen was a great pitcher. Johnny Beazley was a great pitcher. Ernie White. Murry Dickson. You're talking about some pretty good talent there. You cannot win unless you have good pitching. Period. Everything else is immaterial. You've got to have good pitching to win. And good defense helps good pitching. You get a few runs and the pitcher can hold them, the defense can hold them, you're going to give them a battle.

# *Staying Loose*

All pitchers are great competitors. Some people have better stuff than others. Then there were some who were better pitchers when they were drinking than when they were sober, though I won't mention names. Like one pitcher I had, I asked the catcher, "How's old so-and-so feeling in the bullpen?"

He said, "Well, I think he was drinking a little too much last night."

I said, "Send him in. He should be good."

That's a fact, but I won't mention names.

Attitude means a lot when you come in. First of all, you have to throw strikes. If you can't throw strikes, you can't win. And when you throw strikes, as they used to say, throw them low inside, high inside, and don't give them anything to hit. That's pretty hard to do.

# Tim McCarver

21 years (1959–1961, 1963–1980)
Born: October 16, 1941   BL   TR   6'   183 lbs.
Positions: C, 1387; 1B, 103; OF, 15; 3B, 6; DH, 2
St. Louis Cardinals, Philadelphia Phillies, Montreal Expos,
Boston Red Sox

| G | BA | AB | H | 2B | 3B | HR | R | RBI | BB | SO | SB | FA |
|---|-----|------|------|-----|-----|-----|-----|-----|-----|-----|-----|------|
| 1909 | .271 | 5529 | 1501 | 242 | 57 | 97 | 590 | 645 | 548 | 422 | 61 | .989 |

*A two-time All-Star, McCarver played in four decades (eight games in 1959 and six games in 1980). He played in three World Series with the Cardinals (1964, '67, '68), hitting .311 in 21 games. He won Game 5 of the '64 Series with a 10th-inning home run, giving the Cardinals a 3-2 Series lead. In 1967 he finished second in the MVP voting to Orlando Cepeda. He played in three League Championship Series with the Phillies (1976, '77, '78). At Philadelphia, he became Hall of Famer Steve*

Carlton's *"personal catcher." A fine defensive catcher with good speed, he led the league in triples in 1966 with 13, the only catcher ever to do so. In his first year in the minors, 1959, at the age of 18, he hit .360 in 65 games with Keokuk and .357 in 17 games with Rochester before being called up by the Cardinals late in the year. In 1960 he hit .347 in 85 games with Memphis. He finished his career with 82 pinch hits, tying him for 23rd on the all-time list. In 1969 he was sent to the Phillies with Curt Flood, but Flood refused to report. He has been a longtime baseball broadcaster.*

## A Green Rookie

I was 17 years old when I first came up with the Cardinals, just out of high school. My first night on the bench, Henry Aaron was up with a couple of guys. I liked Henry Aaron a lot, growing up.

I let out with one of those, "Come on, Henry!" or something to that effect. Everybody naturally looked at me, and Alex Grammas came over and said, "You know, up here in the big leagues we have a tendency to cheer for our players, not for the opposition."

I was very green, to say the least.

# '64 World Series: 5th Game, 10th Inning

Images remain vivid of that damp, overcast day, that October 12, four days before my 23rd birthday, catching Bob Gibson in Yankee Stadium in a World Series (so many never get there—not to Yankee Stadium or to a World Series). Yet, with my mother's first plane trip, my parents were there to see it, and me, and I somehow saw well the high sinker from Pete Mikkelsen in the 10th inning; the ball headed toward right-center and the air was heavy. The ball had no chance to go out. No chance.

Another image remains: as I neared first base, a huge "7" with his back to me ran toward the fence. If anyone could make the catch, Mickey Mantle could, but even he couldn't; it landed about four rows back. I was numb rounding the bases. I remember touching first and home only, not second and third. . . . Gibson shut them down in the 10th and we led the Yankees three games to two.

More than 30 Octobers have not erased those images. They have, if anything, heightened them—the gray sky, high sinker, the number seven, and, after I'd floated on clouds around the bases, the sight of home plate, dirty and glorious, waiting for my foot to finally come down.

[In the seven-game 1964 Series, McCarver led both teams with 11 hits, batting .478. The Cardinals won the Series.]

# '60 NL Pennant Race

The Cardinals were fighting the Pirates for the pennant in 1960, and we played a game in Philadelphia where Hal Smith got his Achilles cut by Tony Gonzalez on a play at the plate. Hal had about 10 stitches in his ankle, and the only able-bodied catcher was Carl Sawatski. So we go into Pittsburgh to play a five-game series, and Carl Sawatski, in the first game of a doubleheader in the first game there, split his finger wide open, bone exposed and all that. I was only 18 at the time, and I thought I was the only able-bodied catcher. They called Hal Smith in from the bullpen, and he ended up catching with stitches in the back of his ankle. As a matter of fact, I think his stitches even tore during that game. Then they called up Del Rice from their Rochester Redwings, the Triple A affiliate. So I got a few scares during that series.

# Cal McLish

15 years  (1944, 1946–1949, 1951, 1956–1964)
Born: December 1, 1925  BB  TR  6'  179 lbs.
Position:Pitcher
Brooklyn Dodgers, Pittsburgh Pirates, Chicago Cubs,
Cleveland Indians, Cincinnati Reds, Chicago White Sox,
Philadelphia Phillies

| G | W | L | PCT | ERA | GS | CG | SV | IP | H | BB | SO | BA | FA |
|---|---|---|-----|-----|----|----|----|----|---|----|----|----|----|
| 352 | 92 | 92 | .500 | 4.01 | 207 | 57 | 6 | 1609 | 1684 | 552 | 713 | 149 | .975 |

*McLish was an All-Star in 1959, when he won 19 and lost eight for Cleveland, after posting a 16-8 record for the Indians in 1958. After the 1959 season, he was traded with Billy Martin and Gordy Coleman to the Reds for Johnny Temple. In 1960 he was traded with Juan Pizzaro to the White Sox. In 1961 he was traded to the Phillies with Frank Barnes and Andy Carey. Without ever playing in the minor leagues, he pitched with the Dodgers*

*in 1944 as an 18-year-old, then spent two years in the
military in Europe. Between 1947and 1955 he won 102
minor league games, mostly with Los Angeles of the Pacific
Coast League. He hit three big-league home runs, two of
them in 1957 with Cleveland. His given name is perhaps
baseball's longest: Calvin Coolidge Julius Caesar
Tuskahoma McLish.*

# Baseball's Longest Name

My dad named me Calvin Coolidge Julius Caesar
Tuskahoma McLish. I always claimed he was
under firewater when he named me. I was the seventh
of eight kids, and he hadn't named any of them before—that's how the story goes, so I guess it's true—but
I always said I guess he must have been under firewater.

I let that out in one of those train trips. Roscoe
McGowan or one of those writers was always sitting
back there listening. It was kind of a fun thing then,
because the writers weren't mean-spirited; they all knew
what to write. They wrote about the game; they didn't
create controversy like they do now. I'm talking mainly
about the New York writers. But it was fun to know
Gus Steiger and Arch Murray and Roscoe McGowan
and Harold Burr from the old *Brooklyn Eagle*—they
were all good guys.

I get a lot of people who ask me to sign my full
name. I've done it maybe four or five times. How

would you like to get off a subway at Ebbets Field with 50 kids and every one of them asks you to sign your whole name? It'd be the 11th inning before you ever got to the ballpark. I've taken a lot of ribbing about my name, but it's all been good-natured.

## *Pitching at 18*

M y first appearance in organized baseball has to stand out more than any other, because I was 18 years old and I left high school to go play ball with the Dodgers during the war. I was one of the young kids who was brought into baseball at that time. It was either 4-Fs or old men or young kids, you know. I joined them in St. Louis and Leo Durocher brought me in the ball game in the seventh inning with the bases loaded and one out. I'd never thrown a ball in organized baseball in any professional league. I'd never played in the minor leagues. Things got kind of cloudy, because, you know, you're lost. You don't know what you're doing there.

It seemed like they hurriedly got me up. Having never played anywhere, I didn't know how long you're supposed to warm up or how you're supposed to warm up. In those days, you didn't have to throw but 10 pitches. You were ready. Of course, at that time I didn't have a curveball, I didn't have a change-up. I hadn't learned any of that stuff. All I did was just throw fast-balls.

I don't know if I was scared or bewildered. But probably bewildered, because I enjoyed throwing a ball, so I don't think I was scared.

I struck the first hitter out. It was Danny Litwhiler. But then, like I said, it kind of got clouded. Someone bounced a ball over my head and scored a couple of runs, and I don't remember a whole lot more after that.

That game was the start of a 14-game road trip, and we lost them all. McGowan wrote a poem about that 14-day road trip, sung to the tune of "Bless Them All," and my part of the poem was later, in Cincinnati. He said,

> "And in came a kid named McLish.
> Gee, Walker took one healthy swish,
> But why tell the gory
> Details of the story,
> Was fourteen straight games, lose them all."

*Cal McLish*

# The Raise

Aplayer's meal money now adds up to more than our salary. When I signed a contract with the Dodgers in 1944, they gave me a $1500 bonus and a $150-a-month contract. Well, it didn't matter to me what the monthly thing was because I thought I was going into the service. But I don't go in, I don't get my call yet, and I end up joining the Dodgers.

Charlie Dressen [a Dodger coach under Durocher] told me, "Go home and eat a big steak with a lot of butter on it, you're pitching tomorrow."

And I said, "I can't, I just paid my hotel bill."

Dressen said, "Well, you just got paid yesterday."

I told him, "Well, I paid my hotel bill and I don't have any more money."

He said, "What are you making?"

I said, "I'm making a hundred and fifty dollars a month."

So we went into Durocher's office, and they had me meet Mr. Rickey the next morning on Montague Street and he tore up my contract and wrote me one for five hundred dollars a month. So that's how I got started in the money-making side of baseball.

# The Fun Part

When I started playing, all the traveling was by train. That was the fun part. You get to know guys. You get to listen to them talk. If you don't sit around together, you don't know them. We'd always go in the back of the car, like in the men's room, or lounge, they had seats in there. We'd go back there, five or six guys, and listen to Curt Davis talk [a pitcher, came up in 1934, pitched from 1940 to 1946 for the Dodgers] or Whit Wyatt [a pitcher, came up in 1929, pitched from 1939 to 1944 for the Dodgers].

I used to enjoy going on road trips when we'd travel on those trains. They were always pretty short trips—from New York to Boston, New York to Philadelphia, New York to Pittsburgh. The only long trips we had were to Chicago and St. Louis.

The only bad part was that the car was always at the end of Grand Central Station. Leaving and coming, you were always on the trail end and had that long walk, carrying your suitcase. You carried your own bags and you caught your own taxis.

# Bob Oldis

Seven years (1953–1955, 1960–1963)
Born: January 5, 1928   BR   TR   6'1"   185 lbs.
Positions: Catcher (3B, 2)
Washington Senators, Pittsburgh Pirates, Philadelphia Phillies

| G | BA | AB | H | 2B | 3B | HR | R | RBI | BB | SO | SB | FA |
|---|---|---|---|---|---|---|---|---|---|---|---|---|
| 135 | .237 | 236 | 56 | 6 | 0 | 1 | 20 | 22 | 20 | 22 | 0 | .983 |

*O*ldis appeared in two games in the 1960 World Series *for the Pirates. In his final season, 1963, he saw most of his action, appearing in 47 games and batting 85 times for the Phillies as a backup to Clay Dalrymple. He spent four full seasons in the minors before his first big-league appearance, batting between .277 and .289 each year.*

# *Williams: The Scouting Report*

My first trip into Boston, when I was with Washington, I walked across the field and the Red Sox were taking batting practice, and a big number "9" there said, "Hey Bob, how's everything going?"

As you know, it was Ted Williams, and I said, "Good, everything's going good."

He said, "Well, welcome to the big leagues." Something on that order. And he said, "Hey, Bob, you got a pitcher by the name of Pedro Ramos. What kind of pitcher is he?"

I said, "Well, he's got good control, he has a good fastball and a little slider, and he can run like heck."

He said, "His control's pretty good, huh? A fastball pitcher?"

And I said, "Yeah."

So I leave him and I'm walking toward the dugout and Eddie Yost and Mickey Vernon are sitting in the dugout and they said, "Come here. What did Ted want?"

I said, "He wanted to know about the new pitcher we just brought up, Pedro Ramos."

And Mickey Vernon said to Eddie Yost, "See, I told you he wanted to know something about a pitcher."

But I'm just happy to be there. I'm happy that Ted wanted to make me feel like I belonged in the big leagues, that he broke out asking about a pitcher he knew he was going to face later.

# Milt Pappas

17 years (1957–1973)
Born: May 11, 1939   BR   TR   6'3"   190 lbs.
Position: Pitcher
Baltimore Orioles, Cincinnati Reds, Atlanta Braves, Chicago Cubs

| G | W | L | PCT | ERA | GS | CG | SV | IP | H | BB | SO | BA | FA |
|---|---|---|-----|-----|----|----|----|-----|---|----|----|----|-----|
| 520 | 209 | 164 | .560 | 3.40 | 465 | 129 | 4 | 3185.2 | 3046 | 858 | 1728 | .123 | .969 |

*B*orn Miltiades Stergios Papastegios, Pappas is 36th on the all-time list with 43 shutouts, more than Hall of Famers Sandy Koufax and Catfish Hunter; only two less than Whitey Ford, Robin Roberts, and Phil Niekro; and just three behind Bob Feller and Tommy John. He pitched just three minor league games before coming to the big leagues at age 18. He won in double figures in his first 11 full seasons. He had only three losing seasons in 17 years. In 1959, at the age of 20, he went 15-9 with Baltimore, completing 15 of his 27 starts. In 1972 he went 17-7 with *the Cubs with a 2.77 ERA and a no-hitter, the only base runner being Larry Stahl, who reached on a two-out walk in the ninth inning. A two-time All-Star (1962, '65) he was only one NL victory away from winning 100 games in each league. Pappas was a dangerous hitter, and 20 of his 132 hits were home runs, including two in one game in 1961. Baltimore traded him to the Reds with Jack Baldschun and Dick Simpson in 1965 for Frank Robinson, and Robinson won the Triple Crown with the Orioles in 1966.*

# *Perfection*

[On September 2, 1972, Pappas, pitching for the Chicago Cubs, retired the first 26 hitters he faced. The Padres brought Larry Stahl, hitting .226, in as a pinch hitter. Pappas, the best control pitcher in the National League that year, walked only 29 batters in 195 innings. He got a 1-2 count on Stahl, then threw three straight borderline pitches. Second-year umpire Bruce Froemming called all three pitches balls, even though most observers, including catcher Randy Hundley, agreed that any one of the three could easily have been called a strike. Pappas retired the next hitter to get his no-hitter and a 6-0 win.]

I feel that I didn't get what I set out to do. It should have been a perfect game, and to this day, I'm not changing my opinion. I think the umpire was a complete idiot, and I'll think so until the day I die, I guess.

It's stupid that we have that kind of a game and have a call like that, considering the fact when you look at the World Series with Don Larsen on the last pitch he threw—the umpire knew history was being made, he was no dummy. Nobody squawked about the fact that he called strike three and Don Larsen had a perfect game in the World Series.

Any of the last three pitches should have been called a strike. And that last pitch was so close, I mean, you'd need a microscope to figure whether it was a ball or strike; and to have him go the other way and call it a ball and not get a perfect game I think was totally absurd.

## *Lights Out in Atlanta*

One night we were sitting in Atlanta in the Braves' bullpen when I was with the Braves and we were kibitzing down there and talking, and I said to them, "Wouldn't it be funny if the lights went out in the ballpark?" and no more than 10 seconds after that, they had a power failure. The whole ballpark went dark. It was dark for about 45 minutes. When the lights came back on, the guys all looked at me like, "What do you know? The man says, 'Let there be no light, and there the lights go out.'"

They had this Indian out there in left field in Atlanta, Chief Knoc-a-homa, and they had a teepee out

*Milt Pappas (center)*

there. He would come out of the teepee during the game and do a dance and whoop up the fans during the game. Well, one day his air-conditioner had a short in it and his teepee caught on fire. Nobody got hurt or anything, but here's Chief Knoc-a-homa running out of his burning teepee. That has to be one of the funniest things I ever saw in baseball.

# How to Beat the Yankees

The Yankees obviously had very dominating teams back in the late '50s and early '60s; they were the perennial champions year after year after year. They came into Baltimore and swept us the first two games. I was going to be pitching the next game, so a sportswriter, John Steadman, came up and said, "Man, how do you beat these guys?"

It was 11 o'clock at night, I just wanted to get out of there and get home. So I just give him a flip answer, "Well, it's very simple. You shut them out and you hit a home run."

In the afternoon newspaper the next day, the *News American,* Steadman's article talked about the Yankees and how strong they are, how dominant they are, and he said, "Milt Pappas, the pitcher who's pitching tonight against the Yankees, has a very easy theory. He says, 'You just shut them out and hit a home run.' He says that's the way to beat the Yankees."

That night I shut them out and hit a home run and won the game 1-0.

It made all of us look good.

# Herb Plews

Four years (1956–1959)
Born: June 14, 1928  BL  TR  5'11"  160 lbs.
Positions:  2B, 217; 3B, 49; SS, 9
Washington Senators, Boston Red Sox

| G | BA | AB | H | 2B | 3B | HR | R | RBI | BB | SO | SB | FA |
|---|----|----|---|----|----|----|---|-----|----|----|----|----|
| 346 | .262 | 1017 | 266 | 42 | 17 | 4 | 125 | 82 | 74 | 133 | 3 | .959 |

*P*lews hit .270 in 91 games in his rookie season, 1956, with the Senators. He followed that with .271 in 104 games his next season. On September 26, 1958, he participated in five double plays at second base, tying a since-broken major league record. In February 1956, he was traded from the Yankee system with Lou Berberet, Bob Wiesler, and Dick Tettelbach for Mickey McDermott and Bobby Kline. He was traded to the Red Sox in 1959 for

*Billy Consolo. In the minors, he hit .304 for Norfork of the Piedmont League in 1953. The next year he hit .299 for Birmingham of the Southern Association and led the league with 16 triples. In 1955 he hit .302 for Denver, the Yankees' Triple A team, in the American Association.*

## Pete Runnels vs. Ted Williams

Pete Runnels was a steady, good sound ballplayer, and a fine hitter. He could hit the ball to all fields, and he could play several positions too. The year that Ted Williams was battling Pete for the batting championship [1958—Williams beat Runnels .328 to .322], we finished up at home in Washington with Boston, and at the time, I think Runnels was just ahead of Williams. And Dressen made the comment, "I don't want to see anybody walking Williams, I want to see you pitch to him. Make him earn this title, if he's going to beat Pete." Anyway, we had a four-game series with them there, and Pete was hitting the ball on the nose but it seemed like every time he hit it, it was right at somebody. And Williams was ricocheting them off everywhere. And by golly, Ted ended up beating him by a few points. And I never will forget that, that was some exhibition of hitting by both of them.

# Yogi Berra

I've seen Yogi get hit with foul balls in the arms and the shoulders and everything, and he'd be first up to hit in that inning, and he could hit the darnedest ball. You might throw one over his head and he'd hit a line drive, and you might throw one almost in the dirt and he'd do the same thing. Yogi was something else. He always had something to say to you. He always would ask you how things were going for you, you know. He was liable to say anything.

# Embarrassment—and Redemption

There was one time that was pretty embarrassing to me. Eddie Yost wasn't there. It was one of the rare times that he missed a game. I moved over to third base. I had played third base in the minor leagues. In fact, I kind of preferred third base, but I never got much chance to play it in the big leagues. So they put me on third base that night, and we were playing Kansas City. Jeepers, I booted two and threw two more wild to first, and I had four errors before I knew it. Before the game was over, I came up in a crucial spot and hit a double my last time up and won the game for them in spite of all the runs I let in. The next day, Harry Craft, the Kansas City manager, came over to me and said, "Forget those errors. You're too good a ballplayer to let that bother you." He was a good fellow.

# J. W. Porter

Six years (1952, 1955–1959)
Born: January 17, 1933  BR  TR  6'2"  180 lbs.
Positions: Catcher, 91; OF, 62; 1B, 16; 3B, 3
St. Louis Browns, Detroit Tigers, Cleveland Indians,
Washington Senators, St. Louis Cardinals

| G | BA | AB | H | 2B | 3B | HR | R | RBI | BB | SO | SB | FA |
|---|----|----|----|----|----|----|----|-----|----|----|----|-----|
| 229 | .228 | 544 | 124 | 22 | 1 | 8 | 58 | 62 | 53 | 96 | 4 | .983 |

*J. W. (his given name) came up to the big leagues at age 19 and hit .250 that year in 33 games, mostly as an outfielder. In 1951, at age 18, he caught 117 games for Waterloo in the Three-I League and batted .302 with 15 home runs, seven triples, and 95 RBI. In 1952 he hit .340 in 66 games for Colorado Springs in the Western League. He was the American Legion Player of the Year in 1950. Porter is in the American Legion Hall of Fame at Cooperstown.*

191

# In Heaven

I remember arriving
at Old Sportsman's Park in St. Louis
for my first major league game
and thinking they had bypassed the town
and I was at the park in Omaha.
And then came my first look at Yankee Stadium
and knowing that once again I was lost,
but this time the train had stopped
in Heaven.

# '47 World Series

I was in ninth grade when the World Series of 1947
rolled around. The teacher of one particular class
said, "We're not going to study today; we're going to
listen to a baseball game on the radio." She pointed to
me and my chair. She said, "Now the reason we're
doing this is an ex-student of mine who used to sit over
there in Jay's seat may get a chance to play in this
game." It was a little Italian boy named Cookie
Lavagetto.

Well, I don't even have to tell the end of the story.
Bottom of the ninth, two outs, the Yankee pitcher had
a no-hitter, and who was called on to pinch-hit and hits
a double off the right-field fence at Ebbets Field but
Cookie Lavagetto.

I already was into the act of trying to throw things and catch things. I wanted a ball and I wanted a glove and I was peeking through the holes in the fence of the minor league stadium that I walked by every day, to and from school. And then to have that happen, well, it was just like God had pointed down and said, "This is it."

# *John Rice*

[Rice umpired in the AL from 1955 to 1973 and was the plate umpire in a game in Detroit that saw Ray Boone suffer one of his two big-league ejections.]

We were playing the Yankees, the big bad Yankees, in Detroit. Ray Boone was our home run and RBI guy. Unlike his son Bobby and his grandson Bret, Ray had tremendous power. Tommy Byrne was pitching to Ray Boone with the bases loaded. Well, Ray hit the first ever baseball out of Briggs Stadium in left field. Up to this point, no ball had never left Briggs Stadium in left field. But it was about a foot foul.

Stengel went out to the mound and supposedly said to Tommy, "I'm sorry, I know that ball's foul and nothing's happened, but I just can't leave anybody that throws a ball that far out here." So he brings in Tom Sturdivant.

Well, what happened next had to be an accident, because the bases are loaded, and you aren't going to throw a ball at a guy's head with the bases loaded, but that's where the ball wound up. Because of Boonie's crouch and his stance, the bat was kind of above his head. The ball actually just barely missed his head, but it hit the bat and went down third base like a perfect bunt. Fair.

Sturdivant went over to field it, and just as he bent over to pick up the ball, Boone ran right over him. He didn't even run to first base, he just ran to the pitcher. Both teams rush out. A big wrestling match took place—15 minutes of pulling and shoving and screaming and yelling.

When the dust cleared, Boonie and Sturdivant had been kicked out of the game. Reno Bertoia, who was our utility infielder, came up to bat. Stengel came out and asked John Rice, "John, what's going on?"

Rice said, "Foul ball, we kicked Boone out, pinch hitter."

Stengel said, "What foul ball?"

Four umpires missed the play. To this day, that's a foul ball.

*J. W. Porter*

# *Ted Williams: Looking for Revenge*

T he first time Jim Bunning ever pitched to Williams, he struck him out three times, the one and
only time I believe in his career that he was ever struck
out three times in one game. This was the first series of
the year. In those days, it was about a month before you
played a team again. Well, Williams is hitting .450.
[This was 1957. Williams finished the season with a
league-leading .388 batting average. Bunning finished
the season at 20-8.] We talked to guys on the sidelines,
and they said, "That Williams is going nuts."

We said, "What do you mean?"

They said, "Well, he pretends every pitcher is
Bunning. He can't wait to get to Bunning."

That second series, it wasn't Bunning's turn to
pitch in the three games. So another month goes by, we
go back to Boston. Williams is still hitting .420. They
said, "Man, is Bunning going to pitch? That Williams
is driving us crazy."

Well, one of them had the flu, so they didn't meet
that time, either. So another month goes by, and they
come back to Detroit. Ted predicts in the morning
paper, "I'm going to hit three home runs off Bunning
today, including one on the roof." That's in the paper
before the game even starts. We go out there, and the
first time up, he hits a bullet into the lower deck. But
we get two runs. The second time up, he hits a bullet
into the upper deck. Two to two. We get another run.
The third time up, it's the seventh inning, we're ahead
3-2, there's one out, nobody on base.

Jack Tighe was our manager, a very short-time manager. He won't win any awards at all in any of the books, but he stood up—and I was catching the game—he stood up on the dugout step and says, "Walk the big donkey."

Now there's one out and nobody on base. A 3-2 game. That's something you just don't do, walk a guy to bring the lead run up. Jackie Jensen, who leads the league in runs batted in [Jensen drove in 103 for the season] is the next hitter. We walk Williams. Jensen hits into a double play, we're out of the inning.

Top of the ninth rolls around, same identical situation, same identical score. He walks him again. Jensen hits into a double play, we win 3-2. You know, you're supposed to be tossed out of the game if you throw your bat? Williams threw his bat both times, as far as he could throw that sucker. He was so mad.

# Ned Garver

I played with Ned Garver both in St. Louis and Detroit. I have known about half a dozen pitchers in my life who just absolutely knew that pitching was easy. Spahn knew that pitching was easy. Whitey Ford knew that pitching was easy. All he had to do was throw the ball where he wanted to, and he had the advantage.

Well, the average pitcher thinks it's the hardest job in the world. And the harder they work at it, the harder it gets. But if you can go out to the pitcher's mound knowing that the best hitter the other team's got is going to make an out seven times out of 10—if you can just keep that in your brain and walk out there and move the ball up and down and in and out a little bit—you're going to win more games than you'll lose. Garver knew that, and Garver did that as good as anybody. Garver just knew: keep the ball down, make the guy move off the plate occasionally. Spin it up there sometimes. Oh, he was one of one of my favorites.

# *The Greatest Decades*

I hate to get old; everybody hates to get old. But I am so proud of having been there in the '50s. By playing with four different teams in the American League, then going over and finishing up a year in the National League, and all the spring training exhibitions, I got to play with and against some of the greatest ballplayers. I think most historians agree that that decade and the '20s were the two great decades of baseball. They're still doing fine, there's nothing wrong with the '60s or '70s or '80s or '90s, but if you had to separate decade from decade, the '50s would be very near the top.

# Baseball Dreams

*The game itself* is Mother Church,
beyond reproach,
and all us kooks who play,
free agency, etc., etc.,
can't change that.

*Before the game* was limbo, void,
a time suspended,
walking in glue.
If you were lucky enough to be a starter,
the dream began with the last line
of the National Anthem.

*After the game* was when the whoppers began.
A couple of beers and your homer
truly did land "downtown,"
or clear the river and land on the Kansas side.
Your roommate, the pitcher,
was just a couple of breaks away from perfection.

And then your dreams are broken
by a couple of local lovelies . . . .

# Bill Renna

Six years (1953–1956, 1958–1959)
Born: October 14, 1924   BR   TR   6'3"   218 lbs.
Position: Outfield
New York Yankees, Philadelphia Athletics,
Kansas City Athletics, Boston Red Sox

| G | BA | AB | H | 2B | 3B | HR | R | RBI | BB | SO | SB | FA |
|----|------|-----|-----|----|----|----|-----|-----|----|-----|----|------|
| 370 | .239 | 918 | 219 | 36 | 10 | 28 | 123 | 119 | 99 | 166 | 2 | .979 |

*As a Yankee rookie in 1953, Renna hit .314 in 61 games, sharing outfield chores with Mantle, Bauer, Woodling, and Noren. In December of 1953, he was part of the 10-player trade with the Philadelphia Athletics that brought Eddie Robinson, Loren Babe, Tom Hamilton, and Carmen Mauro to the Yankees for Don Bollweg, John Gray, Jim Robertson, Jim Finigan, Vic Power, and Renna. Renna played in 123 games and hit 13 home runs for the*

*Athletics in 1954. In 1955 he played in 100 games for the Athletics. He started his minor league career in 1949 with Twin Falls of the Pioneer League, where he batted .385, drove in 99 runs, and hit a league-leading 21 home runs. In 1951 he led the Three-I League with 26 home runs with Quincy. In 1952 he hit 28 home runs for Kansas City of the American Association.*

# Yogi Berra

When I was traded to the A's and we're playing in Yankee Stadium, I'm up to the plate and Yogi is talking to me before I get in the box.

"How's it going, Bill?" and everything else, so I'm standing and I'm getting ready to hit, standing in the box, and he's giving the signals and he's grabbing some dirt and throwing it on my back foot.

He keeps throwing dirt on my back foot.

I stepped out and I said, "Yogi, darn it, quit throwing dirt on my foot. I'm having a hard enough time up here as it is without you throwing dirt on me."

He was a character.

## *Mantle's Homer off Stobbs*

The home run that Mantle hit in Washington was unbelievable. He was hitting right-handed against Stobbs. Stobbs threw him a change-up and Mickey moved forward just a little bit with his feet, but he held the bat back, which you are supposed to do. He held it back and it was cocked. When he swung at that ball, everything was in motion. What a groove. He hit that ball and it just jumped. I've never seen anything like it. We all came out of our seats and started walking toward the edge of the dugout and looking up, and it just kept going and going. Went right over the clock, high in the left-field bleachers.

They put a little white ball up there, and Charlie Dressen, the Senators' manager, saw it up there for about a month and said, "Get that thing down." 'Cause their dugout was on the first-base side, and he could look right up, and all he saw was that ball, every day. He didn't need that.

# Mike Sandlock

Five years (1942, 1944–1946, 1953)
Born: October 17, 1915   BB   TR   6'1"   180 lbs.
Positions: C, 128; SS, 31; 3B, 25; 2B, 4
Boston Braves, Brooklyn Dodgers, Pittsburgh Pirates

| G | BA | AB | H | 2B | 3B | HR | R | RBI | BB | SO | SB | FA |
|---|----|----|---|----|----|----|---|-----|----|----|----|----|
| 195 | .240 | 446 | 107 | 19 | 2 | 2 | 34 | 31 | 38 | 45 | 2 | .981 |

*S*igned as a catcher, Sandlock played shortstop for the
Dodgers at the start of the 1945 season, then caught
47 games that year, hitting .282 in 80 games. He played
professional baseball for 18 seasons, including time in the
Three-I League, before joining the Boston Braves under
Casey Stengel. He played several years for Fred Haney at
Hollywood in the Pacific Coast League before joining the
Pittsburgh Pirates in 1953, where he caught 64 games

*and hit .231. Knee problems ended his career after his 1954 season with San Diego of the Pacific Coast League.*

## Watching the Babe

When I was 16 years old, my brother took me to Yankee Stadium, and I watched Ruth and Gehrig and Lazzeri and all those guys. I was sitting up in the right-field stands, and Babe hit one right over top of my head, way over—my mouth was wide open and I said, "Boy, would I love just to play there, at Yankee Stadium."

Of course, I never really thought it would happen.

But in 1945, during the war years, I wrenched my knee and  was turned down by my draft board. I asked my board if I could go to spring training with the Brooklyn Dodgers, and they said, "Yeah, you can go." We ended up playing exhibition games at different places, and Yankee Stadium was one of them. I played shortstop in an exhibition game against the Yankees.

It was a pleasure, because as a 16-year-old kid I'm sitting in right field, and now here I am playing in the infield with the big leaguers.

After I played a few innings, I said, "I don't know how Rizzuto could ever make errors in this infield." It was so beautiful, you know.

# *A Hot Time in Pittsburgh*

[Al Barlick umpired for 27 years, including a record seven All-Star games. In 1953 Pittsburgh catcher Mike Sandlock was 38, nearing the end of a long pro career.]

It was about a 118 degrees in the shade in Pittsburgh, one of their hottest days ever. We were playing the Brooklyn Dodgers, and Al Barlick was the umpire. The pitcher was John Lindell, the Yankee outfielder who was enjoying a second career as a knuckleball pitcher. I was catching. It was about 80 feet to the backstop, and during the game, I went back a few times, chasing John's knuckleball, sweating like anything. Everything the Dodgers got their bat on was a base hit. They scored seven or eight early runs and we had to change pitchers.

In about the sixth inning we go out and I come back behind the plate. Barlick and me are both soaked. Barlick says, "You forgot your apron." I had to go back to the dugout for my chest protector. My uniform was so heavy from sweating I didn't even realize I didn't have it on.

Then, all of a sudden, I see John Lindell sitting up there in the stands and he's got what I call a lollipop. You know, something that's got a head on it. He's sitting up in the stands with a nice clean shirt, and I think, "Oh boy, that's where I probably should be sitting, right next to him." While water's sopping out of my shoes because of perspiration, I'm thinking hard, trying to trump up some way to get kicked out of the game.

Hodges is hitting. A good close pitch comes over the plate, and Barlick calls it a ball. I didn't turn around. I just said, "Barlick, does the strike zone change with the color of the uniforms?" and boy, he flew out from back there and swept home plate, and he stuck that little broom right in front of my nose and said to me, "You're not going anywhere."

That's the way it ended up. He wouldn't let me get out. He knew what I wanted.

## *Musial the Pitcher*

I started out as a catcher in the minor leagues in 1938 with Huntington, West Virginia. Stan Musial was a pitcher for Williamson in the Mountain State League. He hurt his shoulder, I guess, but he turned around to be quite an athlete—first base and outfielder—and a great hitter and a great guy. I ran into him several years later in an exhibition game. We were rained out, and as we were going down a ramp, I happened to see him and called out, "Hey, Stan."

He remembered me and said, "Hi, Mike," and we fibbed around a little bit and then he said, "Here, come on with me." He grabbed me by the shoulder and we went into the clubhouse and he said, "Tell these guys what a curveball I had."

"It's like rolling off a table," I said, and I got drowned with wet towels. I'll never forget that. And the thing that impressed me most was that Stan remembered. He was always nice to people, anyway, especially fans.

# Carl Scheib

11 years  (1943–1945, 1947–1954)
Born: January 1, 1927  BR  TR  6'1"  192 lbs.
Position: Pitcher  (OF, 2)
Philadelphia Athletics, St. Louis Cardinals

| G | W | L | PCT | ERA | GS | CG | SV | IP | H | BB | SO | BA | FA |
|---|---|---|-----|-----|-----|-----|-----|------|------|-----|-----|------|------|
| 267 | 45 | 65 | .409 | 4.88 | 107 | 47 | 17 | 1071.2 | 1130 | 493 | 290 | .250 | .966 |

*S*igned out of high school, Scheib was the youngest
player ever to appear in an AL game (16 years, eight
months, five days) when he made his pro debut in 1943.
He went 14-8 with a 3.84 ERA in 1948 and batted .298
(31 for 104). He went 11-7 in 1952. One of baseball's
best-hitting pitchers of his era, he had 57 official at-bats as
a pinch hitter. In 1951 he hit .396 (21-53).

## *The Youngest Ever*

I pitched my first game in the big leagues when I was 16 [in 1943]. I'm still the youngest player ever to play in the American League. The day I signed with the Athletics—my parents had to sign because I was too young—the club told me, "Go down and get a uniform."

By then, the ball club was already out taking infield practice. The game started pretty soon after that. I was in the bullpen, and later on in the game, they told me, "Warm up."

I started warming up, and the next minute they said, "You're in there."

It all went fast for me. We were playing the Yankees that day, and they had a bunch of good ones in those days. It was just the last two innings, I think. But if I remember right, I did pretty good. I got them out, I think. And that was my introduction day.

## *When Bobo Wouldn't Come Out*

Bobo Newsom had a lot of good years. I really don't know why he played for so many teams. I think he was kind of a character and pretty obstinate against the owners or maybe even the managers. He was at the end of his career when he came over to us. Connie Mack's son Earl was the first-base coach, and he didn't know much about baseball. One day Bobo was pitching a pretty close game, getting into the ninth inning, and they thought they'd have a relief pitcher. So Earl walked out and said, "Daddy says to take you out."

Bobo turned around at him and said, "Get out of here."

Earl came in to the bench and said, "Daddy, he won't come out."

Connie said, "Well, leave him in there."

But back then a lot of guys didn't want to come out when they were in a close game in the last inning because there was nothing worse than having a reliever come in and lose it for you. Then you'd say, "Well, I should have stayed in there; maybe I could have done better."

## Knocking Them Down

In our days, you could knock a batter down. That was all in stride. You could knock a guy down and he'd just get up and take it as part of the game.

But sometimes tempers would get hot. One night Saul Rogovin was pitching and Elmer Valo was on second; I think he was the winning run. Little Gus Niarhos was catching. A guy got a base hit into short right field.

Elmer Valo was the type of player, he'd put his head down and never looked at coaches. By the time he hit third base, the catcher had the ball. But this little Gus Niarhos walked up the baseline about six, eight feet. Elmer Valo was a strong man. He just hit him, picked him up, and threw him behind home plate. Niarhos dropped the ball, and, of course, Elmer was safe, and we won the game.

But the pitcher charged Elmer. Elmer had a little cut above his eye, and blood was running in his eye, and Saul Rogovin come in and kinda started punching up underneath him; but by that time, Ferris Fain was out there. And Ferris lowered the boom on him right quick. That was one pretty good fight we had. You didn't hardly see any real fights. Everybody got out there in a mob and started telling jokes, you know. It was part of the game.

# Charlie Silvera

10 years (1948–1957)
Born: October 13, 1924   BR   TR   5'10"   175 lbs.
Position: Catcher
New York Yankees, Chicago Cubs

| G | BA | AB | H | 2B | 3B | HR | R | RBI | BB | SO | SB | FA |
|---|----|----|---|----|----|----|---|-----|----|----|----|----|
| 227 | .282 | 482 | 136 | 15 | 2 | 1 | 34 | 52 | 53 | 32 | 2 | .985 |

*In his first two seasons with the Yankees, Silvera batted .340 in 62 games. He hit .291 in his seven seasons with the Yankees as the backup to Yogi Berra. He caught 20 games in 1952, hitting .327 and fielding 1.000. He was one of only eight players to play on all five of the consecutive world-championship teams, 1949-53. He played in one of the 42 World Series games for which he was eligible. In 1948 Silvera caught 144 games for Portland of the Pacific Coast League, batting .301 with 85 RBI.*

# *Behind Berra*

People say I had a tough break, playing behind Berra, but I don't agree. How many play behind a Hall of Famer? I guess I wasn't good enough to warrant a picture in the Yankee press room, but I was good enough to play on seven pennant winners and six world champions. I didn't hang around because I was Casey Stengel's illegitimate son.

I was involved in two rule-changing plays: In 1949 I was the hitter when Johnny Lindell went out of the baseline and shoulder-blocked Nellie Fox at second to break up a double play. The second rule change was the one to keep photographers off the field. I was interfered with by photographers on the field while going after a pop fly. Photographers ended up off the field.

I played with and roomed with many Hall of Famers, played in New York in the greatest era with the greatest team, and met the finest people anyone would want to meet in his lifetime.

Me, given a tough break? No. I wouldn't trade my career for anything.

## Don't Waste a Stamp

Contract negotiations were always a problem. One year I held out with the Yankees when George Weiss was the general manager. I still have the letter at home. I was holding out maybe for a thousand dollars. He says, "No sense in your spending another three-cent stamp, so sign the contract." And that was it. Didn't have much recourse.

## What They Came to See

Bill McGowan—the umpire they called "number one"—is behind home plate while I'm catching in Boston one day, and Ted Williams is hitting, and of course, he always took the close pitches. I thought we had him struck out one night.

I just said, "Hey, Mac, my goodness."

He said, "Throw the ball back, you blank-blank-blank. They came to see him hit and not you catch."

# Sibby Sisti

13 years  (1939–1942, 1946–1954)
Born: July 26, 1920   BR  TR   5'11"   175 lbs.
Positions:  2B, 359; 3B, 290; SS, 179; OF, 74; 1B, 2
Boston Braves, Milwaukee Braves

| G | BA | AB | H | 2B | 3B | HR | R | RBI | BB | SO | SB | FA |
|---|----|----|----|----|----|----|----|-----|----|----|----|----|
| 1016 | .244 | 2999 | 732 | 121 | 19 | 27 | 401 | 260 | 283 | 440 | 30 | .952 |

*S*isti was the Braves' regular third baseman and second
baseman from 1940 to 1942 before going into the military. In 1946 he hit .343 with Indianapolis and was
named Minor League Player of the Year by The Sporting
News. After his return to the majors, he was one of the
National League's best utility players. He was called "Super
Sub," playing seven positions during his career with the
Braves. He played in 83 games during the Braves' 1948
pennant-winning season. In 1951 he hit .279 in 114

215

games. *He once beat out three bunt singles in a game. Sisti
was a manager in the minor leagues.*

# '48 World Series

In the opening game of the '48 Series [Boston Braves
vs. Cleveland] we beat Feller 1-0. He pitched a two-
hitter and Johnny Sain pitched a four-hitter, and the
big controversial play of the Series was in the bottom of
the eighth inning of that game. Phil Masi was on
second base and I was on first. Boudreau and Feller put
on a pickoff play with Masi at second base. And a
thousand and one pictures I've seen of that play show
Masi diving back into second headfirst, and Boudreau's
putting the tag on him, and he tagged him on his head,
but Phil's hands were still not on the bag, so it's very
obvious that he was out: but the umpire called him
safe. When that happened, I had a good look at it,
being on first, and Johnny Cooney was coaching at
first.

I turned to John and said, "Geez, we got a lucky
break there."

And he said, "We sure did."

Then Tommy Holmes, a pitch or two later, gets a
base hit and drives in Masi and we eventually win the
ball game 1-0. I don't know how true this is, but when
Masi died [in 1990]—somebody told me, now like I
said, I don't know how true this is—but when he left

his will, he said he was out at second base. [Cleveland won the Series four games to two.]

## *Brutal Language at Braves Field*

B raves Field [where the Boston Braves played] was a tough park because the Charles River was in back of the left-field stands and there was a double fence, and the wind invariably blew in from left field. So home run hitters always had a tough time hitting home runs there because the wind would hold the ball up. I heard some brutal language playing second base, because a guy would hit a shot out there and the ball would just hang up and just come back down and the outfielder would catch it. The batter who hit it would think he had one against the fence or over, and by the time he rounded first, he would be cussing to beat the band. It was a tough park to hit in.

## *An Unorthodox Musial*

M usial was a great hitter, no question about it. He could run like heck. He didn't have much of an arm, but hitting-wise—you know he had a very unorthodox stance in the box. I've never seen anybody else try to copy that stance that he had, but he could hit both inside and outside pitches. There was no set way to pitch to him. He was one of the top hitters of all time. [Musial hit 475 home runs without ever leading the league in home runs. He led the league in triples five times, doubles eight times, hits six times, slugging average six times, batting average seven times, runs scored five times, RBI two times, walks once. His career batting average was .331 and he had 3,630 hits.]

# Frank Sullivan

11 years (1953–1963)
Born: January 23, 1930   BR   TR   6' 6 1/2"   215 lbs.
Position: Pitcher
Boston Red Sox, Philadelphia Phillies, Minnesota Twins

| G | W | L | PCT | ERA | GS | CG | SV | IP | H | BB | SO | BA | FA |
|---|---|---|-----|-----|-----|-----|-----|-----|-----|-----|-----|-----|-----|
| 351 | 97 | 100 | .492 | 3.60 | 219 | 73 | 18 | 1732 | 1702 | 559 | 959 | .144 | .978 |

*A* two-time All-Star, Sullivan led the American League *in starts and innings pitched in 1955 and tied Ford and Lemon for the lead with 18 wins. His 2.91 ERA that year was fifth in the league. From 1954 to 1958 he averaged 12 complete games and 15 wins a season. After his first six seasons with the Red Sox, he was 22 games over .500. The American League's tallest pitcher, he was traded in 1960 to the Phillies for Gene Conley, the National League's tallest pitcher. Sullivan pitched four seasons in the minors before joining the Red Sox in 1953. After two years of military service (1951–1952), he had an ERA of 1.78 in 96 innings for Albany of the Eastern League in 1953.*

# Passing the Test

The first batter I faced in the majors was Walt Dropo, when he was with Detroit. The umpire came out to the mound and said to me, "Just get it close, kid, and I'll do the rest."

I threw Walt four strikes right down the middle and the umpire just stared at me as he called all four balls. I didn't say anything, and the rest of the inning went well.

I guess I passed the test.

# The Whole Story

In the 1955 All-Star Game, I got beat in the 13th inning. I went in in the eighth and replaced Ford. An error tied the game, and then I went on to pitch the rest.

I got them out in the ninth, and I pitched the 10th, I pitched the 11th, I pitched the 12th, because only if you pitched in relief could you pitch more than three innings.

And it was the first pitch of the 13th inning—and the thing is, every time they show it on TV, they say, "Sullivan's first pitch—"

They forget I'd already pitched more than three scoreless innings. Everybody thinks I went in for one throw and that was it. [In the 1955 All-Star Game in Milwaukee, the AL led 5-0 in the seventh. Ford gave up two runs in the seventh and three in the eighth. Sullivan replaced Ford with two on and two out in the eighth and the score 5-3. Aaron singled, scoring the runner from second. Kaline's throw got past Rosen, allowing the tying run to score from first. Sullivan shut the NL out in the ninth, tenth, and eleventh. After Conley struck out Kaline, Vernon, and Rosen in the top of the 12th, Musial led off the bottom of the 12th with his game-winning home run.]

I remember coming in afterwards—I wasn't too upset, but hey, I'm not the only guy in the world Musial's hit a ball off of. I threw him an eye-high fastball. He jumped up out of that crouch and tomahawked it out of there. I remember Berra saying later, "Geez, I forgot to tell you, he's a high fastball hitter."

## *Buying New Shirts*

Jack Corbett, with the Red Sox, came over to the Legion ballpark where I was. There was another kid in Burbank named Frank Sullivan, too. Corbett came over to see a left-handed guy named Sullivan, and saw me.

He came to my house and talked to me about signing with Boston. He flew me to Boston. My workout was rained out, but I threw a little bit to Larry Woodall at the park and met a lot of guys.

I'm sitting in the lobby at the hotel and Parnell and Stubbs and McDermott saw me, and said, "Hey, kid, we're going uptown, you want a ride?"

I said, "Yeah," and we jumped in a cab. They went up to an Arrow shirt place, and McDermott walked in there, took off his shirt, put on one and ordered a half dozen others and left the old one, and I thought, "Man, that's pretty neat." That kind of sold me.

# *Hello, Stranger*

I wouldn't have minded the designated hitter. I remember sliding into third once—I finally hit a triple in Boston—and I slid into third, and my old manager from Albany was the third-base coach, Jack Burns, and he walked out to the bag, and he said, "I'd like to introduce myself, I haven't seen you before."

I remember I got a hit once off of Herb Score in Cleveland, and I heard Hegan say, "Oh, no."

I wasn't much of a hitter, so I wouldn't have

*Frank Sullivan*

minded that designated hitter thing. I wouldn't have liked it as a pitcher because the pitcher was somebody I had a chance of getting out.

# A Lot of Trouble

One time in Chicago I had the bases loaded and nobody out, and I was looking down to throw to Minoso, who was at the plate. Sammy [White] called time out, and he came out. I didn't want him too close to me because he used to chew tobacco and spit through his mask, and it was awful. It looked awful.

But I wanted to hear what he had to say, and he came out and he looked over at third, he looked over at second, he looked over at first, and he looked back at Minoso, and then he looked over at me and he took off his mask, and he said, "Geez, you're in a lot of trouble."

We had a lot of fun in those days. Of course, my mouth went off like the Fourth of July half the time.

# Wayne Terwilliger

Nine years  (1949–1951, 1953–1956, 1959–1960)
Born: June 27, 1925   BR   TR   5'11"   165 lbs.
Positions: 2B, 605; 3B, 14; SS, 6; 1B, 1; OF, 1
Chicago Cubs, Brooklyn Dodgers, Washington Senators,
New York Giants, Kansas City Athletics

| G | BA | AB | H | 2B | 3B | HR | R | RBI | BB | SO | SB | FA |
|---|----|----|----|----|----|----|----|----|----|----|----|----|
| 666 | .240 | 2091 | 501 | 93 | 10 | 22 | 271 | 162 | 247 | 296 | 31 | .974 |

*I*n his rookie year with the Cubs, Terwilliger got eight
consecutive hits.  He was part of the eight-player Cubs-
Dodgers trade in 1951, going to Brooklyn with Pafko,
Johnny Schmitz, and Rube Walker for Bruce Edwards, Joe
Hatten, Eddie Miksis, and Gene Hermanski. A star
shortstop in college at Western Michigan University, he
played mainly second base in the big leagues, including
three seasons as a regular—one with the Cubs and two

with the Senators. Terwilliger is a lifelong baseball man, who has coached for several big-league teams, including four years for Ted Williams at Washington and Texas. His highest batting average in the majors was in 1959, when he hit .267 in 74 games with the Athletics.

# *Rhymers*

I sent one of my 'rhymers!' in to Kate Smith—yes, *God Bless America* Kate back in 1939 or maybe '40. It was a war theme . . . a few years later, I was in the Marines in the Pacific. Time does fly by!

Here are some of my other *Rhymers!*:

## My Kind of Guy

*Dropped a ball I shoulda caught*
*With the bat went four for naught*
*Picked off first in inning eight*
*But heck we won . . . let's celebrate!*

## "Play Ball"

*Shoes got holes, no sandwich sacked*
*Ball all scuffed . . . bat's cracked*
*Glove needs a web, no jock or cup*
*Where's the field . . . Batter Up!*

## Saturday Morning Bravado

*Hi Mom, just juice, game starts at eight*
*Big one today so can't be late*
*Got beat last week, 19 to none*
*Guarantee we'll win this one!*

# '51 NL Pennant Race

I was traded to the Dodgers in mid-season in 1951. The last day of the season, the Giants had already won, so we had to win our game in Philadelphia. Talk about pressure games. We had been ahead the whole season, practically; now we're behind by a half game and it was a one-run game. The last of the eighth inning in Philadelphia. The score was tied, the bases were loaded, and Eddie Waitkus—I'm on the bench, naturally—and Eddie Waitkus hits a line drive up the middle. Robin-son makes a diving, lunging grab just off the ground to his right, catches the ball, and that ends the inning. And he laid there on the ground. The trainer went out, and he laid there for quite a while, and Cookie Lavagetto came over to me on the bench.

He said, "Maybe you'd better go down to the bullpen and start throwing."

I said, "You're kidding me!" I said, "No way am I going to move off this bench until they push me down there." Anyway, Robinson got up and jogged off the field. He'd knocked the wind out of himself. Then, in the top of the ninth, he hits a home run to eventually win the game. And that was exciting, to see a guy like Robinson, who could do it anyway, and to be there and to watch him perform under the greatest of pressure both in the field and at bat. That was exciting.

## Be Glad to Take It

My first game in the big leagues was against Boston: I struck out on three pitches against Johnny Antonelli, a left-handed pitcher. He threw three fastballs by me. I had good swings on them. That was my first time at bat. I think my second game I got a bloop base hit to right field. Johnny Hopp was playing first base. I remember that. I remember him saying, "Congratulations." And I said, "That was really a great hit, wasn't it?" He said, "Son, you take it. You'll be glad to take it later on, too."

## Baseball Visions

I still see . . . . *Ted Williams* in his first appearance after coming back from Korea in 1953 when I played second base for Washington . . . he hit four line drives that game, two over my head and two over Mickey Vernon's—

*Willie Mays* playing with the best all-around talent and with great enthusiasm—

A nude *Frank Howard*—sans his front partial (teeth) leading the Washington Senators with his version of the "Nats" fight song . . . 1969 . . . after a win!

*The 1951 playoff game in the Polo Grounds,* and falling off the equipment trunk in the dugout as I twisted to follow Thomson's home run slip over the left-field wall . . . and then not quite sure what happened!

*Mickey Mantle's* home run climb almost in slow motion and then level off as it disappeared next to the scoreboard in left-center in old Griffith Stadium . . . 1953.

*Jackie Robinson*—the toughest player and probably the smartest . . . at least on the bases, where it took a dozen throws sometimes in a rundown, and if you got him, you were lucky . . .

*Ted Williams'* final at-bat . . . who but No. 9 could end his playing career the way he did . . . . I still get a chill when I see films of that last swing.

# Frank Thomas

16 years (1951–1966)
Born: June 11, 1929   BR   TR   6'3"   200 lbs.
Positions: OF, 1045; 3B, 394; 1B, 271; 2B, 4
Pittsburgh Pirates, Cincinnati Reds, Chicago Cubs, Milwaukee
Braves, New York Mets, Philadelphia Phillies, Houston Astros

| G | BA | AB | H | 2B | 3B | HR | R | RBI | BB | SO | SB | FA |
|---|----|----|---|----|----|----|---|-----|----|----|----|----|
| 1766 | .266 | 6285 | 1671 | 262 | 31 | 286 | 792 | 962 | 484 | 894 | 15 | .971 |

*T*homas was a three-time All-Star. From 1953 to 1962 he hit 20 or more home runs nine times; he hit 30 or more three times. Twice he drove in over 100 runs. In 1954 he hit .298 in 153 games for Pittsburgh, with 23 home runs and 93 RBI. In 1958 he hit 35 home runs with 109 RBI for Pittsburgh. He was involved in a 1959 trade with the Reds that sent Burgess, Haddix, and Hoak to the Pirates. Thomas hit 34 home runs for the 1962 Mets team that lost 120 games. In that season, he hit two homers in each of three consecutive games. In the minor *leagues, he twice led his league in RBI (132 in 1948 and 131 in 1952). He hit a total of 100 minor league home runs.*

## Catching Bare-handed

I could catch anybody's fastball bare-handed. I did that as a dare in 1949 with a pitcher by the name of Bill Pierro. We were in the outfield, and he was popping off, saying how hard he could throw, and I said, "I'll catch your fastball bare-handed," and he said, "No, you can't."

I said, "Well, let's get 60 feet six inches. But what I want you to do first is go down to the bullpen first and warm up, 'cause I don't want you to—"

He said, "No, you can't catch it even if I don't warm up." So I caught two, and he said, "I'm not warm."

I said, "Well, I knew you'd say that. Go down to the bullpen and warm up."

So he did that, and I caught five in a row, and that kind of deflated his ego a little bit. And that's the reason why I did it. I did it more on a dare because of that. [Pierro came up to the Pirates the next year, but pitched only 12 big-league games, losing his only two decisions.] I look back now and say, "I was kind of crazy for doing it." But when I was a kid, everybody used to have a glove, and I used to play shortstop in fast-pitch softball without a glove because I couldn't afford one. So my hands were toughened up, and I knew what I was doing. If I thought there was a chance of my getting hurt, I wouldn't have done it. I said to everybody who wanted to throw hard that I would catch it. "You throw the ball across the seams, and you throw it as hard as you can." Because when you throw the ball across the seams, the ball is going to stay straight. I told them I would catch the fastest ball that they could throw.

Probably the toughest one I had to catch was Don Zimmer. He drew a line 60 feet six inches, went back about 20 feet, ran up to the line and threw me a spitter. When I caught it, he threw his glove up in the air and said, "You made a believer out of me." He probably threw as fast as anybody I ever caught. [Zimmer was a big-league infielder for 12 years, before becoming a longtime major league manager and coach.]

So I was crazy for doing it, but I knew what I was doing.

## *My First Love*

Baseball was always my first love. Mom said I never went to bed unless I had a ball and bat in my crib. I gave everything that I had to baseball. The greatest thrill for me was just putting on a major league uniform and staying as long as I did in the major leagues, because every boy has that dream, to become a major league ballplayer, to reach the top, the pinnacle, and I did that.

# Bobby Thomson

15 years (1946–1960)
Born: October 25, 1923  BR  TR  6'2"  180 lbs.
Positions: Outfield, 1506; 3B, 184; 2B, 9; 1B, 1
New York Giants, Milwaukee Braves, Chicago Cubs,
Boston Red Sox, Baltimore Orioles

| G | BA | AB | H | 2B | 3B | HR | R | RBI | BB | SO | SB | FA |
|---|----|----|----|----|----|----|----|-----|-----|-----|-----|-----|
| 1779 | .270 | 6305 | 1705 | 267 | 74 | 264 | 903 | 1026 | 559 | 804 | 38 | .973 |

*A three-time All-Star, Thomson hit perhaps the most famous home run in baseball history on October 3, 1951; the three-run homer off Ralph Branca ended the National League season, giving the Giants a dramatic playoff victory over the Dodgers and clinching the NL pennant. He hit 20 or more home runs eight times. He had four 100-plus RBI seasons. He hit 32 home runs in the Giants' 1951 pennant-winning season. His switch to third base that year allowed Willie Mays to take over in center field. He was traded to Milwaukee in 1954 with Sammy Calderone for Johnny Antonelli, Don Liddle, Ebba St. Claire, and Billy Klaus. In 1957 he was traded back to the Giants with Danny O'Connell and Ray Crone for Red Schoendienst. He was born in Scotland.*

# A Feeling for the Fans

I started out riding the trains, and played with fellows like Al Dark and Eddie Stanky. We sat around and kicked baseball around. We talked baseball. It was only natural that we were closer together then. So I don't know, maybe these guys talk a lot of baseball among themselves in the locker room, but that's a little different.

And of course, it depends who's on your ball club. When you have guys like Al Dark and Stanky and Whitey Lockman and pitchers like Sal Maglie and Larry Jansen, we thought we played intelligent baseball. And of course, with Durocher there, we were going to be aggressive and were generally one step ahead of the other guys as far as I was concerned.

But I don't want to separate us from all the players from the past.

I had a lot of feeling for the fans. I always felt we owed the fans, our fans, a good ball game. I remember one Sunday on a hot day, we lost a doubleheader. The stands were full, and I felt terrible. I thought, "Gee, these poor people could have been out at the beach having a good time, and we let them down."

## *Keystone Kops*

I opened up 1947 at second base. Mel Ott was managing, and he put me there. I'd never played second base. I was just trying to make third base in competition with a couple other guys. Walker Cooper was catching, Bill Rigney was in there, and we got beat; we didn't do anything right. A little pop fly between the catcher and pitcher, they bumped into each other and landed up on the ground. I remember there was a runner on first base, and I guess he stole second. Bill Rigney was playing shortstop and I'm playing second, and Walker Cooper just threw the ball right over second base, which he is supposed to do, but probably I was supposed to cover, but I didn't get the sign from Bill. I missed the sign, whatever, and the ball went into center field. It must have been three or four things like that, and we got beat. Just a lousy ball game. And we walked in the locker room and it was very quiet. It had been so ridiculous. And Rigney and I looked at each other and we burst out laughing. I remember that. I mean, I've never come close to anything like that again, certainly not when Durocher was managing.

# *It's All in the Timing*

The next spring, 1952, after that playoff home run against the Dodgers, we were losing to the Cards by three runs in the last half of the ninth; and with two outs, bases loaded, I hit a grand slam. I mean, if that had happened at another time, to win a pennant or something, that's the ultimate. With two outs and the bases loaded, three runs behind. But when those things happen in the middle of the season, people don't remember them long.

# Virgil Trucks

17 years (1941–1943, 1945–1958)
Born: April 26, 1919   BR   TR   5'11"   198 lbs.
Position: Pitcher
Detroit Tigers, St. Louis Browns, Chicago White Sox,
Kansas City Athletics, New York Yankees

| G | W | L | PCT | ERA | GS | CG | SV | IP | H | BB | SO | BA | FA |
|---|---|---|-----|-----|----|----|----|----|----|----|----|----|----|
| 517 | 177 | 135 | .567 | 3.39 | 328 | 124 | 30 | 2682.1 | 2416 | 1088 | 1534 | .180 | .955 |

*T*rucks pitched 35 career shutouts, 72nd on the all-
time list. He is one of only four pitchers to pitch two no-
hitters in a single season (1952); he won both 1-0. Ten
times he won 10 or more games in a season. He had a
complete-game win in the 1945 World Series, after pitching in only one regular-season game (without a decision),
making him the only pitcher to win a World Series game
after not winning a game during the regular season. A
two-time All-Star, he won 20 games in 1953 and 19 in
1949 and 1954. In the minor leagues, he won 65 games

and had four no-hitters. In 1938, Trucks' first minor league season (at age 19), pitching in Andalusia in the Alabama-Florida League, he went 26-5 with a 1.25 ERA. His 418 strikeouts—in 273 innings—are the second-highest total in the history of professional ball.

# The No-Hitter That Almost Wasn't

[Virgil Trucks is one of only four pitchers to have pitched two no-hitters in a single season. The others: Johnny Vander Meer, Allie Reynolds, and Nolan Ryan. A disputed call at first base by Bill Grieves in an August 25, 1952, game almost kept Trucks out of the record books.]

In the third inning of my second no-hitter, Johnny Pesky, our shortstop, had trouble getting off the throw on a ground ball by Rizzuto. Bill Grieves called Rizzuto safe at first. We all thought he blew the call. The official scorer, John Drebinger, first ruled it an error, then changed it to a hit. He said it was a hit because the ball got stuck in Pesky's glove. Others in the press box said it should have been ruled an error.

I had the one-hitter going into the seventh, and Drebinger phoned the dugout to ask about that ground ball. Pesky told him the ball didn't stick to the webbing, he just couldn't get ahold of it cleanly. They announced over the PA system that Rizzuto's hit had been changed to an error.

Grieves told me, "You've got your no-hitter. Go get it."

I told him, "You so-and-so. I'm not worried about a no-hitter; I'm trying to win the game. Besides, if you hadn't blown the call at first, they wouldn't have had to decide what to call it."

I'd retired 19 in a row when I faced Berra with two out in the ninth, trying to hold on to a 1-0 lead. He hit a line shot to Al Federoff at second base, hit so hard Berra couldn't even leave the batter's box. A foot or two to either side and it would have been a hit. So everything turned out okay.

# A Strange Year

1952 was a strange year. I was 5-19, but it could have been the other way around just as easily. We didn't score many runs. [Detroit finished last at 50-104. Though Trucks' ERA was 3.97, Detroit was last in runs scored, averaging just 3.6 runs a game.] I pitched two no-hitters, a one-hitter, and a two-hitter. Three of my five wins were 1-0.

My first no-hitter was against Washington. More people have told me they saw that game than actually were there. [Attendance was 2,215. The time of the game was a speedy 1:32.] Bob Porterfield pitched a great game himself. He held us hitless for five and two-thirds innings. In the ninth inning I struck out Mickey Vernon for the final out. But the game still wasn't over. There was still no score going into the last of the ninth. Then, with two out, Vic Wertz hit a home run to win it.

I almost had three no-hitters in 1952. A month after my no-hitter against Washington, they came back into Detroit, and the first pitch I threw, Eddie Yost hits a clean single between George Kell and the shortstop. I retired the next 27 batters and won another 1-0 ball game.

I knew Eddie Yost was a first-ball hitter. If he didn't swing at the first pitch, generally he walked. That was a rule—and the way pitchers knew him, and the way pitchers functioned. I got a little lax, I guess, and didn't put as much as I should on the ball, and he hit it. It was a clean base hit; there was no doubt about that.

And I had another close call. After the first no-hitter against Washington, I pitched six and two-thirds innings against Philadelphia before they got a base hit, and it was the only base hit they got. Hank Majeski got that base hit.

So I had a lot of close calls where there could have been other no-hitters. But when you're playing, you're not expecting to pitch no-hitters—you're just trying to win a ball game.

## *Eddie Rommel*

[Rommel was an American League umpire for 22 years after twice leading the AL in wins as a pitcher. In a 1932 game, he gave up 29 hits and eight walks in 17 innings of relief pitching—and got the win!]

*Virgil Trucks*

I always got along with umpires, because those are the people who could make you or break you, and I knew that. The first encounter I ever had with them was when I was with Detroit and we were playing in Fenway Park in Boston. The stands come right out practically on the field. It was a real hot day, and I had pitched the day before. I've got this bucket and I'm pouring it up and down the floor of the dugout to help cool things off. Kell was playing third for us and leaned into the stands to catch a pop foul. A fan took it out of his hands. The umpire called, "No catch." While they're arguing, Birdie Tebbetts took the bucket out of my hands and threw it out on the field. Eddie Rommel came over and threw me out of the ball game. I told him, "I didn't throw the bucket." But he threw me out anyway. I was upset because I'd never been thrown out of a ball game in either the minor or major leagues.

After the game, I went to see him because the umpire's room was near our dressing room. Rommel saw me, and he's smiling right away. He said, "Look, I'm not going to turn you in, it's not going to cost you 25 dollars." Twenty-five dollars was a lot of money in those days. He said, "I've got to report it, but you're not going to get fined. I had to throw somebody out of the game when the bucket came out onto the field. Everybody saw you with that bucket. I'm not hurting the ball club by throwing you out because you pitched yesterday; you're not going to do anything for the ball club."

I understood what he was saying—he had to throw somebody out—and since it didn't cost me anything, I said, "Okay, that's fine with me."

# Bill Virdon

12 years (1955–1965, 1968)
Born: June 9, 1931   BL   TR   6'0"   175 lbs.
Position: Outfield
St. Louis Cardinals, Pittsburgh Pirates

| G | BA | AB | H | 2B | 3B | HR | R | RBI | BB | SO | SB | FA |
|---|----|----|----|----|----|----|----|-----|-----|-----|-----|-----|
| 1583 | .267 | 5980 | 1596 | 237 | 81 | 91 | 735 | 502 | 442 | 647 | 47 | .982 |

*V*irdon was signed by the Yankees and went to the
Cardinals in 1954 in the trade that sent Enos
Slaughter to the Yankees. In 1954 he led the International
League in hitting with a .333 mark while hitting 22
home runs and driving in 98 runs for Rochester. He was
the National League Rookie of the Year in 1955, batting
.281 with a career-high 17 home runs for the Cardinals.
The following year he was traded to the Pirates after 24
games for Dick Littlefield and Bobby Del Greco and hit
.334 in his 133 games for the Pirates. Four times Virdon

*hit 10 or more triples in a season, leading the league with
10 triples in 1962; he was also a Gold Glove winner that
year. In the Pirates' 1960 World Series triumph over the
Yankees, he sparkled in the field. It was his ground ball
that took the bad hop in Game 7 and hit Tony Kubek in
the throat, opening the door for the key runs that made the
Pirates' comeback victory possible. In 13 years as a major
league manager with the Pirates, Yankees, Astros, and
Expos, his teams had a record of 995-921. He was twice
named* TSN *Manager of the Year (in 1974 with the
Yankees and in 1980 with the Astros).*

# *Hitting Casey*

I was with the Yankees in spring training 1954, working
with the outfielders: Mantle, Bauer, Woodling, and
others. We were fielding balls and making throws. It
was my turn; I fielded the ball and threw.

Somehow Casey Stengel had moved between me
and the relay man, and I proceeded to hit him in the
back with my strongest throw. It knocked the wind out
of him, and by the time he got his composure back I
had got back amid the other fielders, hoping he
wouldn't know who did it.

Casey's comment was, "If you guys could throw
that accurate in the game, you might throw someone
out."

I was traded later. I guess he knew.

## *The '60 Pittsburgh Pirates*

Two instances in the '60 World Series that come to mind are the bad hop that hit Kubek in the throat, really the break we needed. After the bad hop, we scored five runs. You have to think that someone was looking out after us. I hit the ball that hit Kubek in the throat. I hit the ball well, but if it had not taken a bad hop, it was a routine double-play ball. And if it doesn't take the bad hop, we've got two outs in the eighth inning and we're down 7-4. Most instances, you don't win when you get in that situation. That doesn't mean we wouldn't have won. 'Cause usually that club found a way to score some runs enough to win. But I have to say, that was one of the breaks that we needed to win the Series.

The first game of the Series—I led off the first game, and we were losing 1-0. Maris had hit a home run in the top of the first. But I led off the bottom of the first and I walked. Dick Groat and I hit-and-run a lot. He put on the hit-and-run sign and then took it off and I didn't see him take it off. I went on the pitch and Dick took the pitch and Yogi Berra threw the ball and nobody covered second, and I went to third and we scored three runs after that. I have to think that was a break. [The Pirates won the game 6-4.] So I can look back at those two instances that I was involved in that were important.

# Wally Westlake

10 years (1947-1956)
Born: November 8, 1920   BR   TR   6'  186 lbs.
Position: Outfield (3B, 34)
Pittsburgh Pirates, St. Louis Cardinals, Cincinnati Reds,
Cleveland Indians, Baltimore Orioles, Philadelphia Phillies

| G | BA | AB | H | 2B | 3B | HR | R | RBI | BB | SO | SB | FA |
|-----|------|------|-----|-----|-----|-----|-----|-----|-----|-----|-----|------|
| 958 | .272 | 3117 | 848 | 107 | 33 | 127 | 474 | 539 | 317 | 453 | 19 | .978 |

*I*n his first five big-league seasons, Westlake averaged 21 home runs and 83 RBI. He hit for the cycle twice with the Pirates. In 1951 he was traded with Cliff Chambers to the Cardinals for five players, including Howie Pollet and Joe Garagiola. He hit .330 in 82 games for Cleveland in 1953. On the Indians' pennant-winning team in 1954, he played in 85 games. He began his minor league career in 1940. He spent 1943–1945 in military service. In 1946 *he hit .315 for Oakland of the Pacific Coast League. He was on the NL All-Star team in 1951.*

# '54 AL Pennant Race

A day in 1954 provided one of the most trying periods of my life on the playing field. I'm with Cleveland and we're battling the Yankees for the pennant. We're playing the Yankees a doubleheader on Sunday, maybe 86,000 people in the ballpark, and I'm playing in the second game. It's the last of the eighth inning and we're behind 2-1. Tommy Byrne is pitching for the Yankees. There are two outs, runners on second and third, and I hit a double off the left-center-field fence, but I realized I'd missed first base.

Well, I'm dying out there. Eighty-six thousand people out there—man, I was saying Hail Marys like I never said them before. I'm on second base with what would be a double to drive in the tying and winning runs, but if they call for the appeal at first base I'm out and we're still behind 2-1. But nobody appealed it— once the pitcher makes the pitch, they can't appeal.

You might remember a few years back, Miller had those advertisements—advertised their beer with all those old jocks. Remember the one with Boog Powell and the umpire, Jim Honochick? Well, Honochick was umpiring first base that day, and when I was on second base, the next hitter—I think it was Larry Doby—

popped up. I went in, got my glove, and when I ran by first base, old Honochick looked at me and he said, "Hey, partner. Touch that thing next time you come by." He knew I missed it.

I got in the outfield and I really took a deep breath. This was late September 1954; I think we had about two weeks to go. It was a crazy schedule. The Yankees came in, we were leading the league by something like four and a half, five and a half games, with two weeks to go, and the Yankees came in to play a Sunday doubleheader. And if we win that doubleheader, which we did, the Yankees were out of it, and they were. I've often thought, suppose that they did win that second ball game because of my mistake. Anything can happen in two weeks. Sometimes there's not much difference between hero and goat.

# Gene Woodling

17 years (1943, 1946–1947, 1949–1962)
Born: August 16, 1922   BL   TR   5'9 1/2"   195 lbs.
Position: Outfield
Cleveland Indians, Pittsburgh Pirates, New York Yankees,
Baltimore Orioles, Washington Senators, New York Mets

| G | BA | AB | H | 2B | 3B | HR | R | RBI | BB | SO | SB | FA |
|---|----|----|----|----|----|----|----|-----|-----|-----|-----|------|
| 1796 | .284 | 5587 | 1585 | 257 | 63 | 147 | 830 | 830 | 921 | 477 | 29 | .989 |

*W*oodling was an All-Star in 1959. He played on
*five world-championship teams with the Yankees, 1949–*
*1953. He batted .318 in 26 World Series games and is*
*10th on the all-time list for both World Series walks and*
*runs scored. After the 1954 season, he was part of the 17-*
*player trade between the Yankees and Orioles that brought*
*Don Larsen and Bob Turley to the Yankees. In 13 big-*
*league seasons he played in more than 100 games, batting over*
*.300 five times. His career high in both batting, home runs,*
*and RBI came with Cleveland in 1957 (.321, 19, and 78).*
*He hit 10 or more home runs nine times. A great defensive*

*outfielder, he committed only 35 career errors in over 3,000 chances. He won four minor league batting titles with averages of .398, .394, .344, and .385. With San Francisco of the Pacific Coast League in 1948, he not only led the league in hitting with his .385 mark, but he also had 202 hits, 107 RBI, and led the league with 13 triples. He spent two years in the navy during World War II.*

## Invisible Batting Coaches

There is no such a thing as a hitting coach. That guy upstairs says you're going to hit when you're two years old, you'll hit when you're 90. If he don't, forget it. You know, batting coaches are always around when a guy's hitting .300. You never see them when a guy's hitting .150.

## Which Guy?

You judge a player on whether he can win—not just on the statistics. There are lots of guys who'll hit you 30 home runs, knock in 125 runs—five of them will mean something to winning. And you've got a .265-.270 hitter who'll drive in 60 runs, and maybe 35 or 40 of his runs have something to do with winning a ball game. Which guy would you rather have?

## *Eighty-Dollar Millionaire*

I made $80 a month in the minors. Guys say, "You played pro ball for $80 a month?"

I say, "Heck, yes. I was a millionaire."

Guys in rubber shops in Akron, they were making $12 a week. Here I was, making $20 playing baseball. And you know, there's always one thing I can say: If there's a better way to earn a living, you show me.

## *Batting Practice*

I started two minor leagues after the season started and led them both in hitting. I'd never picked a bat up until after the season started. I never took batting practice my latter years. Of course, I didn't do it on my own. I asked Paul Richards, and he said, "Hey, you've been around as long as I have. You do what you think is right. You're playing every day, and you're doing a good job." So I didn't do it to be a smart guy or anything like that. I got his approval. So I never took batting practice and had great years. If batting practice made you a better hitter, everybody would hit .999.

## *Better with Age*

My last four, five years were my best in the big leagues. I can't explain why. Well, I guess you

*Gene Woodling*

could say I got better with age. I'd have liked to got better when I was 20.

## *A Piece of Good Luck*

To say you played baseball for a living—I just shake my head. It was just a piece of good luck.

## *Homering for the Chief*

When I was with the Yankees, every time we'd come into Cleveland, we'd draw seventy-five, eighty thousand people at that stadium. I'm from Akron, Ohio, so Cleveland was more or less my hometown. In July of 1954 [July 12] Reynolds and Feller hooked up in a no-hitter one evening. Chief ended up pitching a no-hitter. Feller ended up pitching a two-hitter. Along about the 8th inning I had hit a home run, and that was it, so we won 1-0. It was a wonderful thing for Chief, a wonderful thing for me, because it was at home. You always like to do well at home. I played a long time, played with winners, played with losers, but this one game stands out. I probably know more ballplayers than anyone living because I played with seven different clubs. Chief pitched another no-hitter that year, in Yankee Stadium, and I hit a home run in that one too, but it wasn't the only run. [On September 28, Reynolds no-hit the Red Sox 8-0.]

# Al Zarilla

10 years (1943–1944, 1946–1953)
Born: May 1, 1919   BL   TR   5'11"   180 lbs.
Position: Outfield
St. Louis Browns, Boston Red Sox, Chicago White Sox

| G | BA | AB | H | 2B | 3B | HR | R | RBI | BB | SO | SB | FA |
|---|-----|------|-----|-----|----|----|-----|-----|-----|-----|----|------|
| 1120 | .276 | 3535 | 975 | 186 | 43 | 61 | 507 | 456 | 415 | 382 | 33 | .974 |

*A*n All-Star in 1948, Zarilla twice hit over .300 in the
big leagues. His .299 average in 1944, his first full
*season, helped the Browns to their only pennant. His .329*
*mark in 1948 was fourth in the AL. His .325 in 1950*
*was fifth in the league. In 1950 he had four doubles in*
*one game, tying a major league record. A solid hitter and a*
*good outfielder, he played in over 100 games for eight*
*straight years. He coached for Ted Williams at Washington.*
*He played in the minors for five years before coming up to*
*the Browns, hitting over .300 in four of those seasons. He*

*was traded to Boston in 1949 for Stan Spence. In 1952 he was traded with Willie Miranda to the Browns from the White Sox.*

## The Biggest Hurt

I can almost see it in slow motion, that ball Jerry Coleman hit in the eighth inning of that Yankee-Red Sox showdown in 1949, the last game of the season, with the winner going to the World Series.

They beat us 5-2, the killer coming when, with the bases loaded and two outs, Coleman hit a dunk fly ball down the right-field line and I had to go all out. I had to catch it or else, because everybody was running.

I missed the darn thing by two inches or so, and people don't realize that I popped all the blood vessels in my left knee. I was in the hospital for 10 days when I got back to Boston, and even Mr. Yawkey and Joe Cronin didn't know it that I hurt myself that bad.

But the biggest hurt was losing that game.

## Start Swinging

If you can't hit the fastball, you're not going to be in the big leagues, period. That's the name of the game. I was a first-ball hitter, and the pitchers knew it. If they threw a fastball close, I'm swinging. Because that's my strength, and because I had a hard time hitting the changes, which most everybody does—changes and curveballs.

Actually, you know, if he's a fastball pitcher, like Bob Feller—you know he's going to throw you a hard fastball, a hard curveball. Bob Lemon, Early Wynn, the Newhousers, they went right at you. And if you don't hit their best pitch, you're not going to hit. If he's a curveball pitcher, look for the curveball.

And if he's got three pitches, just start swinging. 'Cause you're in trouble.

## Coming to Play

We traveled by train, and we'd play cards in the men's room. We were just a happy bunch of guys. We enjoyed playing, and I'll tell you one thing: When we came on the field, we came to play.

## Going Five Hundred

One year with the Browns I made three errors all year. They all came in the same inning. But the Browns had that hard outfield, like playing on concrete.

That same game, I got three hits. Even the manager said, "Well, you're even, Al. You're actually 500 for the game, three and three."

## *Running on DiMaggio*

Just playing against Joe DiMaggio was something. He had that bad heel one year. He was playing center field, and I know he wasn't full speed. I got a base hit right through the box toward him, and when I rounded first base, I saw he wasn't getting to the ball like he usually did, so I just kept on going. He looked up and he saw me, and I just made it to second base. He almost got me.

So when the inning was over, as I was going to right field and he was coming across toward his dugout, he said, "You'll never do that again, you little jerk." And he laughed. We're both jerks, you know.

But that stands out, because Joe was a real quiet person.

# Gus Zernial

11 years (1949–1959)
Born: June 27, 1923   BR   TR   6'2 1/2"   210 lbs.
Position: Outfield  (1B, 35)
Chicago White Sox, Philadelphia Athletics,
Kansas City Athletics, Detroit Tigers

| G | BA | A B | H | 2B | 3B | HR | R | RBI | BB | SO | SB | FA |
|---|----|----|---|----|----|----|----|-----|----|----|----|----|
| 1234 | .265 | 4131 | 1093 | 159 | 22 | 237 | 572 | 776 | 383 | 755 | 15 | .968 |

*A*n All-Star in 1953, Zernial hit more home runs in
the 1950s than any American Leaguer except Mantle
and Berra. On October 1, 1950, he hit four home runs in
a doubleheader at Comiskey Park, the only player ever to
do so. In 1951 his 33 home runs and 129 RBI led the
league. That same year he hit a record-tying seven home
runs over a four-game period. In 1953 his 42 home runs
were just one behind Al Rosen's league-leading total. From

*1950 to 1957, he averaged 28 home runs and 86 RBI per season. In 1958 he had a league-leading 15 pinch hits for Detroit, hitting .395 as a pinch hitter. From 1946 to 1948 he hit .333, .344, and .322 in the minors with 41 home runs for Burlington of the Carolina League, and 40 home runs and 156 RBI for Hollywood of the Pacific Coast League. He was part of a three-club trade in 1951 that sent him to Philadelphia with Dave Philley and Minoso from Cleveland to the White Sox. In 1957 Zernial was traded to the Tigers with Billy Martin, Tom Morgan, Lou Skizas, Mickey McDermott, and Tim Thompson for seven players, including Bill Tuttle, Duke Maas, and Frank House.*

# *My Idol*

I was born and raised in Beaumont, Texas, and they had a Detroit Tiger farm club. They had guys who went up from there like Rudy York, Hank Greenberg, Roy Cullenbine, Benny McCoy, Hal Newhouser, Virgil Trucks, Dizzy Trout. I was a kid in the knothole gang, only about 15, and most of these guys were about only 19 or 20. So I followed that club, and one of my idols was Newhouser. Now, Hal was a great pitcher, and he's never been given a lot of credit because he pitched during the war years, but let me tell you—this guy was a pitcher. He could throw.

It was the late '30s when I'd followed those guys in Beaumont, and I played my first big-league game in

Detroit in 1949, and who was on the mound? Hal Newhouser. And I tell you, I looked at this guy, and it was a childhood kind of a dream. Here I'm facing a guy I idolized when I was a kid. Now, I'm no longer a kid, but I'm facing this same guy. I remember talking to Appling.

I said, "Hey, Luke, what does this guy throw?"

He said, "Other than aspirin tablets, he's got a pretty good curveball."

The very first time I went to the plate, as I recall it, he threw three pitches, and I don't think I saw any of them. They were all strikes. He beat us 4-1, I think. We only got three hits. Appling got one of them, I got the other two. But my first time at bat, I went down on strikes to a guy I idolized as a kid. It was Newhouser.

## *Trying to Jack It Out*

As a minor league ballplayer, I could hit the home run and I still could hit for average. I think the only thing I regretted about my career is that I didn't concentrate more on getting the base hit when I should have gone for a base hit rather than trying to go for a home run.

You're hitting in the bottom of the ninth or the top of the ninth and you're behind, and I tried to jack one out once in a while when I should have gone for a base hit. I think I could have been a better average hitter. I was a .340 hitter in the minors, and I ended up being about a .270 hitter in the big leagues.

I think I was a better hitter than my average shows. Of course, I can say that now because I don't have to prove it.

## *Can Anything Else Go Wrong?*

In 1954 we were getting trounced in a game in Philadelphia. Back in those days, they used to water the fields by attaching hoses to spigots that they would have buried in the outfield. They'd put a rubber cover over them, but this particular day, I knew that that cover was off that sprinkler. You know, you're just aware of what's around.

But we were getting beat so bad—it was like 17-0 and we were in the top of the ninth inning, playing in Philadelphia—and the fans were all over us, you know, balls flying everywhere and I'd probably misjudged a couple of them. But I said, "I'll catch the next ball that's hit out here, no matter what happens."

Billy Consolo hit the ball into left-center, and I stepped in that hole where that water spigot was. It tripped me and I went down and landed on my left shoulder and broke it. Heck, I didn't even catch that ball. It hit me in the leg after I tripped.

# *Turning It Up a Notch*

Philadelphia was enjoyable for me. We didn't win the pennant, but I played with some excellent ballplayers. [In 1952, Zernial's first full season with Philadelphia, the Athletics finished fourth, four games over .500.] Bobby Shantz was just one of the finest young pitchers I'd ever played with in my life. Alex Kellner was equally as good. Joe DeMaestri was an excellent ballplayer at shortstop. Dave Philley was a good center fielder. Ferris Fain, an excellent hitter. Elmer Valo. Pete Suder. I enjoyed my four years in Philadelphia playing with what I figured were ballplayers about as good as you could play with. Unfortunately, we didn't win, but those were good years, good-feeling years.

We would play even with the Yankees for seven innings and we'd be in the ball game. But when you had to turn it up a notch, we didn't have that notch to turn it up. The Yankees always had that notch. When they went into the seventh inning, they said, "Hey, fellas, we got two innings, we got to win this ball game," and there was that notch they could turn it up to. We never had that notch. I think that's the biggest difference. I think that's why the Yankees won, because you could play the Yankees even with decent pitching and the good ball clubs, and a lot of us did. But when the Yankees came to the eighth and ninth inning, they took the field as a different team. Just that one notch made the difference, and they beat you.